COACHING FROM ESSENCE

COACHING FROM ESSENCE

Create a Thriving Practice
Doing Powerful Work
with Clients You Love

ROBERT ELLIS

Published by Futurosity

Visit our websites:
www.futurosity.com
www.coachingfromessence.com

Copyright © 2023 by Robert Ellis

First edition 2023
All rights reserved.

No part of this book may be used or reproduced in any manner without permission in writing from the publisher, except in the context of reviews.

*For my beloved Michèle,
who won't let me be anything less
than my best self.*

*And for the clients and coaches
I have been privileged to work with,
who let me coach from my essence.*

CONTENTS

I
GOOSE IN A BOTTLE
Goose in a Bottle   *1*

II
PATHS AND QUESTS
Paths and quests   *7*
Gravity   *17*
The Love Threshold   *21*
You Are the Solution to a Problem That No Longer Exists   *27*
Levels of Creation   *31*
The Futurosity Continuum   *37*
Optimize for serendipity   *45*
How to Knock Over the Empire State Building   *49*
Begin Before You're Ready   *51*

III
FORM AND ESSENCE
Form and essence 55
Find Your Essence 59
The Essential Choice 67
The Essence Questions 69
What You Were Born to Do 73

IV
THE RED PAPERCLIP
The Red Paperclip 77
Create Clients You Love 79
Show, Don't Tell 83
Dream Together 85
Create a Coaching Alliance 89
Boundaries 95
Clients and Friends 99
Coach Above Your Level 103
Be a One Room Schoolhouse 105
Give Yourself Away 107

V
BE THE HOST
Be the Host 111
What You Know in YOUR Bones 117
Six Coaching Questions 121
The Wayfinding Question 125
The First Three Sessions 127
The Answer is in the Question 131
Duchamp's Door 133
Speak Your Client's Language 137

Evocation and Provocation   *141*
How (Not) to Give Advice   *143*

VI
THE DARK ALLY
The Dark Ally   *149*
Turn Toward Everything   *153*
Our Work as Human Beings   *163*
A Good Day   *167*
A Major Chord   *169*
Failing by Succeeding   *171*
Give Everything to Everything   *173*
The Advanced Practice   *177*

VII
THE ULTIMATE PRACTICE
The Moment Inside the Moment   *183*
The Ultimate Practice   *187*

VIII
ENDNOTES
Endnotes   *193*
Acknowledgments   *199*
The Coaching From Essence Program   *201*
About the Author   *203*

COACHING FROM ESSENCE

I

GOOSE IN A BOTTLE

A man will be imprisoned in a room with a door that's unlocked and opens inwards; as long as it does not occur to him to pull rather than push.
—Ludwig Wittgenstein

GOOSE IN A BOTTLE

There's a zen riddle that goes something like this:
Take a baby goose and put it in a glass bottle. Pull the neck through the neck of the bottle so you can feed it. Feed the goose until it's too big for the bottle.
There are two rules:
You can't kill the goose.
And you can't break the bottle.
Here's the riddle:
How do you get the goose out of the bottle?

People will come to you for coaching for any number of reasons. It's usually because of an intractable problem, often with another person. It may be a project they need help with or a process they want to improve. It could be a pattern they've noticed (they keep recreating the same problems, or several people have given them feedback about behavior that's not serving them). A difficult passage may have them stumped. They may be seeking to clarify their purpose.

[COACHING FROM ESSENCE]

How do you get the goose out of the bottle?
Put it on a diet?
No, it's already too fat. The bones are too big. It won't come out.
Melt the bottle?
You don't want to cook the goose!
I'll give you a hint. . . .
You're the goose.

Clients come to you because they don't like where they are, or they don't know how to get to some place they'd rather be. And there are good reasons for their dissatisfaction or confusion. Some of those reasons are outside of the client—challenging circumstances—and some are *inside* the client.

Or, rather, the client is inside some of the reasons they aren't living the life they long for.

They're inside their bottle.

You're in a bottle, too.

The bottle tells you what things mean, what's true, what's desirable, what the future looks like.

It tells you what's *possible*.

Okay.

I don't know the Zen answer, but here's one answer:
Break the fucking bottle.

Who says you have to follow the rules? Where do the rules come from anyway?

All those beliefs about who you are and what will make you happy, what success looks like, and all your fears about failure and what you have to do to avoid it—that's your bottle.

All those beliefs you have about what coaching is and who you are as a coach, and how to create a practice you love—those, too, are your bottle.

Think you can only charge like a therapist, maybe a couple hundred dollars a session? Bottle.

Think you can only charge by the session, not on retainer? Bottle.

Think you can't charge money if you're a new coach? Bottle.

Think you shouldn't coach for free? Bottle.

Think you need to be certified to be a coach? Bottle.

Think you need a degree to be a coach? Bottle.

Think you need to be older, more experienced, a white male, etc., to coach executives or be a successful coach? *B-O-T-T-L-E.*

We help clients break their bottles.

This book will show you how to break your bottle.

II

PATHS AND QUESTS

*We must let go of the life we have planned,
so as to accept the one that is waiting for us.*
—Joseph Campbell

PATHS AND QUESTS

Let's keep this simple.
All you're trying to do is get from A ... to B.

A   B

A is where you are now.
B is what you want to create.

B can be anything: the solution to a problem; clarification of your essence or purpose; a change in feeling, mindset, or behavior; or the creation of a billion-dollar business. No one comes to you for coaching because they want to stay at A. If they do, then *staying at A* is their B.

To get to B, you first need to know what B is. That requires *clarity*. Getting clear about B is a better place to start than A. B is where you want to be, and where you want to be shouldn't be limited by where you are.

Once you know where you want to be, it's helpful to know

[COACHING FROM ESSENCE]

where you are. That requires *honesty*. You have to tell the truth about A. If you want to get to New York, it's helpful to know that you're in San Francisco and not Los Angeles; otherwise, you're going to end up somewhere in the Atlantic Ocean.

So.

What's the most important thing you want to create in your life right now?

What's your B?

Now, if you've thought of something that you want to create in your life, something that's important to you, we have to ask, *Where did that B come from?*

Have you ever had your heart broken?

I've posed this question to numerous audiences. Everyone raises their hand. But the real question is, *What did you learn from heartbreak?*

When I ask people what they've learned from heartbreak, the answers vary widely. Someone will say, "I should have protected myself more." And someone else will say, "I shouldn't have protected myself so *much*. I should have been more open."

What did *you* learn from heartbreak?

I'm not suggesting that heartbreak is the same for everyone, but everyone experiences heartbreak. And yet, what you learned is different from what everyone else learned. Why did you learn something different? Because you *chose* to learn something different.

We choose what to learn from our experiences.

Sometimes we choose the wrong lesson. Maybe it's the right lesson—at the time—but the lesson becomes obsolete. We have experiences, decide what they mean, and then create our future based on those choices. In other words, *most of the time we're actually creating the future from the past.*

[PATHS AND QUESTS]

If you ask most people what they want to create, they'll tell you a Bonsai version of their dream, a beautiful miniature version of what they actually want. Or they'll tell you a dream that isn't really theirs—it's their mother's or father's or spouse's or kid's or friend's or employer's. It may even be a dream from their past self—something they used to want or something they think they're supposed to want (but they only *want* to want it).

Often, it's something they already know how to create; it's just a recycled goal they already know how to achieve, but in a different form.

In my experience, once you start working with a client on B, their B changes, partly because they don't really know what they want.

"I want you to help me find the shortest path to becoming an extraordinary leader," my client says.

"That's great," I say. "What do you want to lead?"

"I don't know."

"Then you're not on a path," I say. "You're on a quest."

If you're doing something you already know how to do, if you're recreating something you already know how to succeed at, then you'll probably end up at B or somewhere similar to B.

If you know where B is and where A is, then you're just looking for the shortest distance between two points. That's a project management challenge.

You're on a *path*.

You need a pathfinder, a project manager. That's called *management*.

[COACHING FROM ESSENCE]

Everything is familiar. It's like being on a guided tour. *On the right is what I already know how to do, and on the left are some things I've already done, now with a different coat of paint applied.* Yes, it's a journey, but it's not a very interesting one.

You don't want to be on a tour. You want to be on an *adventure*.

So, you don't actually want to get to B.

As Yogi Berra said, "If you don't know where you're going, you'll probably end up somewhere else." You *want* to end up somewhere else, *but somewhere better than you can imagine when you set out from A.*

Let's call that *B-prime*.

Since you don't want to get to B, B is not your goal. It's an *aim*. You aim for B—the best B you *can* imagine—but you're really looking not for the life you have planned but for the one that's waiting for you.

Since you can't imagine it, you don't really know where B-prime *is*. You may not even know where *A* is. There is no path.

You have to go on a *quest*.

To be on a quest, you must know how to journey into the unknown. You need to embrace uncertainty. If things are certain, there are few possibilities. When things are uncertain, the situation is full of possibilities. Anything can happen. You need to learn how to navigate the unknown, to befriend uncertainty.

That's called *leadership*.

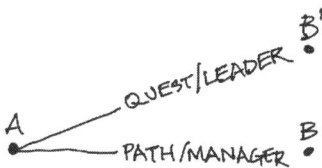

You are not a leader unless you are guiding people through the unknown to something better than they can imagine when they begin their journey. If you know where you're going and how to get there, you're a tour guide.

To be clear, you're always on one or more *paths* somewhere in your life and business—and you should also be on one or more *quests* somewhere in your life and business.

The only way to create B-prime is to risk creating something less than what you want. Let's call that *B-sub*.

Some people call that *failure*.

I call it a *lesson*.

The faster you can learn, the faster you can create B-prime. You create B-prime by conducting experiments and by creating rapid feedback loops.

There's another possibility: *drifting*. If you are not creating—even if only a B you already know how to create—if you are not on an adventure, learning and growing, you're adrift.

You don't want to drift.

[COACHING FROM ESSENCE]

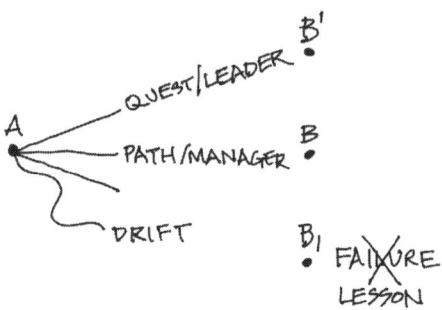

Our role as coaches is to help our clients create B-prime—something that is better than they could imagine for themselves when they began to work with us.

Every good Quest starts with a good Quest(ion).
Let me give you a personal example of what I mean.
At the end of 2014, I experienced a heartbreak that sent me into a dark passage. I experienced not only emotional heartbreak but physical heartbreak, too. In 2016, I had two heart operations for atrial fibrillation, an electrical malfunction of the heart. Almost every day for these two years, I would wake in the morning and ask myself, *How did this get to be my life?* I had somehow managed to create the exact opposite of everything I thought I wanted.
One day I had an epiphany: *I was half-hearted everywhere in my life.* I had one foot in and one foot out of my relationship. No wonder it imploded. I was a hired gun in my work, showing up and doing only what I was paid for. My work was transactional; I wasn't building relationships. It was the same with my friends and family. It was a harsh awakening.
So I started my Quest with this Quest(ion):
How can I be wholehearted?

[PATHS AND QUESTS]

I became intentional about showing up, as much as I could, with my whole heart. I made new friends (and I was astonished they would be friends with me, something I am eternally grateful for because I was in a very dark place—I didn't even want to be around me). I completely reinvented the way I work as a coach (which has become Coaching From Essence), and I focused on creating relationships with my clients, doing deep personal as well as professional work. When I was ready, I started dating again, showing up as my wholehearted, imperfect self.

The results were better than B—I discovered B-prime. I met Michèle, my extraordinary beloved, in 2017, and we married a year later. My coaching practice is full of clients I love. I now make more money than ever (multiple six-figures), and my full practice includes only about a dozen clients (a third of whom have been pro bono because I love working with early-stage founders and entrepreneurs).

While a path is predictable or easily discoverable and repeatable, a quest is unpredictable (once it has been discovered and becomes repeatable, it's a path).

Knowing where to start when you're on a quest is hard. As Joseph Campbell wrote, "You enter the forest at the darkest point, where there is no path. Where there is a way or path, it is someone else's path."

As coaches, we are allies on the quest. We have to help our clients find their own paths.

I always start by helping my clients articulate their Quest(ion). What is it that's missing? What are they longing for? What is the life that is trying to be lived through them? What are their tropisms? (Tropisms are what we naturally turn toward, the way plants naturally turn toward the light.)

[COACHING FROM ESSENCE]

The next step is to help them become comfortable with the unknown, to embrace uncertainty. They have to have the mindset that they are embarking on an adventure. They are putting themselves in the way of serendipity, of unforeseen possibilities. Now we are creating from the future, where dreams and possibilities are not dictated by what was possible in the past.

Once a client has clarified their Quest(ion), I can think of no better advice than this quote from Lewis Carroll: "If you don't know where you are going, any road will get you there." I encourage them to take any road.

When you take a road, you don't have to travel down it very far to know whether or not it is leading you in the direction of your longing. If it gives you life, it's easy to see it. When I work with clients who have begun a quest and are headed in the right direction, it's always visible on their faces. You can feel energetically that they have found a thread. A road that lights them up may become their path—or lead to another road that does.

I emphasize to my clients that there is no failure on this quest. It's not possible. You either get your B (something you were after or something equally satisfying), or you get B-prime (something better than you could have imagined when you set out from A—we are always helping the client optimize for this), or you get a lesson and a new road to try. It's impossible to fail if you are paying attention.

If the road doesn't light them up, they still learn something. We can also help them understand the lesson (and find the light) by helping them notice what the journey is bringing them.

Especially in my first several sessions, I will open the session by asking the client, "What's different? What's different since the last session? What's different since we first started working together?" What we pay attention to grows, and what goes

[PATHS AND QUESTS]

unnoticed withers. If they can notice some positive change, however small, we can amplify it. That's food for the journey.
So.
What's your Quest(ion)?

GRAVITY

IF YOU LOOK at our diagram, those dots below A and B look like planets.

A is kind of like Earth. It has a lot of gravity. B might be the moon. The moon doesn't have much gravity. If you're on Earth and want to get to the moon, you need a lot of energy to escape the Earth's gravity. A rocket burns more than half its fuel just to get out of Earth's atmosphere. It takes a lot of energy to get out of your comfort zone.

The moon's gravity—your B's gravity—is about one-sixth as powerful as Earth's, or A's gravity. That feels about right. A's gravity is much stronger because it has more mass, the weight of all your experiences, and all your choices about what your experiences mean. B's gravity is less, but the more it resembles something you've already done, the more attractive it is because it's familiar and comfortable.

What about B-prime?

B-prime doesn't have much gravity; it doesn't have much mass. It's something you've never done before, something you don't know you can do. It doesn't exist yet, and it's unlike anything that existed before.

You can't imagine it.

B-prime may have little gravity—it may have *antigravity*. It may be attractive, but it may also be scary. This is one of the reasons you begin going after what you want with such optimism and enthusiasm—and then find yourself recreating B, back on the path, instead of pursuing your quest.

As coaches, we need to think like astronauts. There's very little gravity in space. When we work with a client, we need to help them leave A's gravity and find more space, the space to dream their real dream, the life that longs to live through them.

Sometime after the halfway mark of a mission, astronauts often encounter the *third-quarter effect*. Mood and morale suffer. It's likely that at some point in your client's quest, they'll find themselves bored, challenged, uncomfortable, or distracted. They'll want to give up on you, their dream, or themselves. The work may conjure up their *Dark Ally*. That's when you need to remind them why they're here and what called them to this journey. They told you their dream, you believed them, and even though that dream may (and most likely will) evolve on their quest, it's your responsibility to help them stay true to their dream—and their essence.

They may also experience the *overview effect*, which happens when astronauts look back at Earth and realize that it's all one planet. When you are 238,855 miles in space and look back at Earth, you see how everything is connected. You begin to see that so much more is possible for you and for everyone. You may be inspired to idealism. That's a good thing. That's gravity for B-prime. Help your client be an idealist.

Finally, be careful not to let your client get a case of the *space stupids*. The lack of gravity, the usual ways you orient yourself—and stress—can all affect your vision, thinking, and mood. You need at least fifteen percent of the earth's gravitational pull to maintain your sense of up and down in space. Don't let them neglect their responsibilities while they pursue their quest.

Remember, you're creating a space with *little* gravity, not a space without *any* gravity at all. Create a safe space for your client to dream as well as a safe space for them to face hard realities where you question, challenge, and ground their truths.

THE LOVE THRESHOLD

What does gravity look like?

When you leave A and set out for B, you'll have to pass through several *thresholds*, forces that want to keep you from creating what you truly want, what's calling you.

Some of us flirt with answering the call.

We dance back and forth.

Sometimes we're not sure the call is right for us. But usually, we hesitate because we're afraid. To leave the world you know, to leave the known for the unknown, is an act of faith. It requires surrender and commitment.

When you are on the cusp of embarking on your quest, standing at the threshold between the life you know and the one calling you, you will have to face the voices.

There will always be people who will say—whatever it is you long for—that it's not possible for you. You will have to face the Guardians of the Gate. They will say, *You can't come in. You're not smart enough. You're too smart. You're not old enough. You're too old. You don't have any experience. That's not possible, not legal, nobody wants that, it's a dumb idea.*

Some of these voices will come from outside—from parents,

spouses, friends, employers—and some, the most insidious Guardians of all, are *our voices of doubt*.

We gather allies on our journey, friends and colleagues and mentors who support and guide us. We also have allies inside us—our dreams, skills, what we know in our bones, our essence. And we also have saboteurs whispering in our ears, trying to keep us safe. Trying to keep us *in place*.

In my work with hundreds of clients, I've noticed several thresholds. Thresholds feel like *barriers* when you encounter them; they feel like walls, limits you can't overcome. But a threshold is not a wall; it's *a doorway*. It's a place to notice, pause, learn what you can, and then pass through.

There are a handful of thresholds you're almost sure to encounter on your quest.

SILLINESS

The first threshold is what I call the *Silliness* threshold. It's the fear of not looking good. If you start to pursue something you want, especially something you've never done before, something you may not be very good at, you have to go back to being a beginner. You may be going after something that other people—people whose opinions you care about—don't value, even though it's important to you. You may not look perfect initially. You may be less confident and afraid of losing your status.

That can stop you from embarking on your quest before you even start. You hit the Silliness threshold, shut down, and nestle back in A, where it's safe.

When I'm coaching someone, I know when we're getting close to their true dream because they almost always laugh when they talk about it. They'll discount it, giving me all the reasons it's not practical or possible for them.

If you think you're silly for wanting what you truly want, you've hit the Silliness threshold.

KNOWLEDGE

If you make it through the Silliness threshold, the next one you'll likely encounter is the *Knowledge* threshold. You either know too much or not enough. We choose what we learn from experience, and what we know from experience determines what we think is possible for us and what we think we should pursue. You may think of something you want, but if you know too much about it, you'll think it will never work. You'll *know* it will never work because, after all, you have all the experience to know why it *won't* work, why it's not a good idea. You can become an expert at why you'll never have what you want.

Maybe you don't know *enough*. You want something aspirational, something you've never done before. You start believing it might be possible for you, and then you realize you don't know anything about it. And *not knowing* becomes an excellent reason to stay at A, where things are familiar and safe.

TRUST

We're hardwired to keep ourselves safe. If you've passed the Silliness and Knowledge thresholds, the next stop is often the *Trust* threshold. You're willing to take a risk, to step into the unknown, but—is it safe? What if you get hurt?

The space between A and B-prime is unfamiliar territory. It

can feel very vulnerable. You may not know how to create safety for yourself. If you are on a quest for something more aspirational, something that will require collaboration or partnership with people that are new to you, how do you know if you can trust them?

SANITY

The *Sanity* threshold is the fear that if you go after what you want, you'll be completely overwhelmed. I coach a lot of entrepreneurs, some very early-stage entrepreneurs. At some point, almost everyone I've worked with has had to cross the Sanity threshold. They fear they're in way over their heads. They're on the verge of losing everything. A constellation of emotions rises and threatens to engulf you: fear, uncertainty, confusion, exhaustion, and doubt.

LOVE

All of these thresholds ultimately lead to the most important one: the *Love* threshold. The Love threshold is the fear that if you knew the truth about yourself, you would discover that there is something fundamentally wrong with you—that you're unlovable. And the fear that, even worse, *someone will find out*.

These thresholds don't necessarily happen in the order I've described, and you may not experience all of them. But all of these thresholds and more lay between you and the life that's calling you.
And they are all lies.

[THE LOVE THRESHOLD]

They are forms—thought forms—that have nothing to do with your essence. As coaches, our work is to help our clients navigate these thresholds, disentangle themselves from these forms, listen to what calls them, and follow their longing.

YOU ARE THE SOLUTION TO A PROBLEM THAT NO LONGER EXISTS

I WAS HAVING a conversation with a friend. We were sharing tales about our past, talking about our fathers.

When there was a lull in the conversation, he looked at me and said, "You know, your father is dead."

"Huh? I know."

"No," he said, "You don't understand. Your father is dead."

"What?" I said. "I know. He died in 1976."

"You're not listening," he said. "Your father is dead."

I looked at him with a blank stare.

"You don't have to try to make him proud of you anymore."

You are still trying to solve the unsolvable problem of your past. And it keeps you from creating what you truly want.

What problem are you trying to solve? — *lovable, worthy, capable*

At the deepest level, it's the Love threshold. You learned at a very early age to become something you're not in order to be loved.

You created strategies to keep yourself safe because it wasn't safe to follow your essence. You had to protect yourself. You had to hide your pain. You learned to look out for yourself, to look good in front of others, to be on the lookout for what you needed before someone else got it.

Above all, *you learned how to survive.*

Self-interest, status-seeking, scarcity, and survival.

All of us learned these lessons early in life. Even if you were fortunate enough to have parents who tried to teach you something different, you learned these lessons from your family, your teachers, your friends (and television, magazines, the internet . . .). It's the invisible soup we simmer in, the hidden curriculum we are all taught.

It started when you were a kid.

When I was a kid, I wanted to be an artist and a writer.

My father didn't value either of those things. I'm not faulting my father. He didn't understand art and writing. He worked for the Fuller Brush company, selling industrial cleaning supplies (I didn't understand industrial cleaning supplies). He was always encouraging me to learn something practical. He would say, "How are you going to make money as an artist and a writer?"

For a long time—even long after he died—I continued to do his work for him. I would ask myself, "How am I going to make money as an artist and a writer?"

And so, to be loved by my father, I didn't make art, and I didn't write. I did things that had nothing to do with who I was. I learned how to sell. I thought that would make him proud of me (the good thing is, *I learned how to sell*).

I also became a rebel. Rebellion is a great place to hide your pain. The strategy is simple: *pretend it doesn't hurt.*

All of this meant that I went on a long detour in my life before I could come back to myself and create a form that matches my essence.

I don't need my father's love now. The irony is, I always had it.

[A PROBLEM THAT NO LONGER EXISTS]

Being the solution to a problem that no longer exists produces a tension between *creating from the past and creating from the future*.

You're still trying to survive something that happened to you in the past instead of creating something out of the future, out of future possibilities, something congruent with your essence.

If you ask someone what they want, what their B is, many people will give you a B that they think would solve a problem they *had* that no longer exists. If you really get them dreaming, they'll give you a B they believe will solve the problem that no longer exists *once and for all*.

But it won't.

When a client presents a grandiose dream—one that is simply *bigger* than their life now—it's often an attempt to finally solve the problem that no longer exists once and for all. A true dream is not grandiose; it's *resonant*. It may be big, and it may require a personal transformation, but its defining quality is that it feels authentic to the person and their essence.

You want to create from the future and help your clients do the same. To create from the future, you need to do the work of unraveling your outworn strategies for staying safe.

The decisions you made to survive served you when you made them.

You're here. You made it.

But even though your decisions served you, your understanding of the conditions you based them on may or may not have been *true*. And even if it was true then, it may or may not be true *now*. Most likely, it's not true now.

Your decisions may be obsolete.

You've outgrown them. You don't need to be afraid to express an opinion that somebody else might not like. No one is going to send you to bed without dinner. You're no longer in danger of not surviving.

What's more, the problem you're solving *may never have existed*.

A sad reality of human relationships is that they're fraught with disconnects (what my beloved, Michèle Taipale, calls *perplexities*).

When you have a disconnect, you make up a story.

And then you have to protect yourself from the story you made up. You develop a limp from the imaginary pebble in your shoe.

And before you know it, you're a goose in a bottle.

LEVELS OF CREATION

On your journey to the future you're creating, you have a handful of tools to work with. You can arrange these tools in a hierarchy, with each level affecting the other levels. I call these *Levels of Creation*.

Some levels are more obvious than others. Some happen within yourself. Let's call those your *inner game*. Some are about how you take action or manage people or resources. Let's call those your *outer game*.

You can think of the Levels of Creation as a backpack full of creative tools:

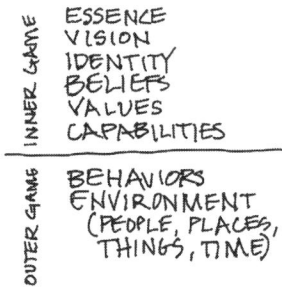

At the top is your *essence*, and then your *vision* or *purpose*. Who are you and what do you want to create?

Next is *identity*. Your identity is the sum of your beliefs about yourself. Do you see yourself as a visionary? A coach? A leader? An entrepreneur? Who do you need to become to be the person who does what you want to do? Become the kind of person who can create what you want to create.

Examine your *beliefs*. To a large extent, your beliefs determine what's possible for you. People tend to act in a way that's congruent with their beliefs about themselves and the world—and you're no different. But most of us don't examine our beliefs to see if they're helping us or hindering us.

Identify your *values*. Your values reveal what's important to you. Do you have the right priorities to create what you want?

Know your *capabilities*. Do you have the knowledge, skills, and abilities required to create what you want? You can hire someone with the capabilities you're lacking, but there are also capabilities you will need to have or develop yourself in order to reach your vision.

All of that is the inner game. The inner game is the inner work you have to do for yourself. Many people don't think about the inner game, which is one reason they can't produce the results they want in the outer game. They have an identity or hold beliefs that aren't congruent with what they say they want, or they lack the necessary beliefs or capabilities to reach their aims.

The outer game is about the *behaviors* or actions you need to take—what you need to do—and the *environment*, or the outer world, that consists of people, places, things (i.e. resources), and time. Do you have the right people (or the right relationships), are you in the right place, have all the resources you need, and is it the right time to create what you want?

You can work from the top down or the bottom up. In other

[LEVELS OF CREATION]

words, if you commit and pursue a clear vision and purpose, it will change who you are, your beliefs, your values, and so on. But you can also change the people you hang out with, the places you go, and your behavior, which will influence your capabilities, values, beliefs, and the sense of who you are.

You can also start at the level where you have the most leverage. Maybe changing your beliefs will provide the biggest shift. Maybe you're not taking enough action. If you are working on the right level, you'll see results.

It can be immensely helpful to take an inventory of your Levels of Creation:

—Are your vision and purpose clear, compelling, and congruent?
—Do you believe you're the kind of person who can succeed at what you're aspiring to do?
—Do you have any untrue beliefs that are holding you back?
—Do you have the necessary values and priorities, or are any of your values in conflict with one another?
—Do you have the knowledge, skills, and abilities you need to accomplish your aim? If not, can you hire them? How can you acquire them yourself?
—Are you taking the right action? Are you taking enough action?
—Do you have the right people, are you in the right place, and do you have the resources to do what you want? Are you allowing enough time? Is right now the right time?

If you have all the right things on each level, if you have enough of the right things, if the levels are aligned with each other, and if you're taking consistent action, then it's just a matter of time before you have what you want. If succ possible, success is assured—in time. But you've got work to do if things are not right, enough, and aligned. The levels can help you pinpoint where to focus.

Working on these levels is straightforward if you're conscious and intentional about how you apply them. If you're not, there are several gaps or conflicts within the levels that can cause problems:

Integrity gaps. Integrity gaps are misalignments between your values and your behaviors. If you aren't walking the talk, you're unlikely to create the desired results. This is one of the most common leadership traps.

Knowing-doing gaps. Some people know what they need to do, they're capable of doing it, but they won't take action. Why don't they do what they know to do? There are lots of possible reasons, including holding onto an identity, beliefs, or values that are not right, enough, or aligned in a way to help them create what they want to create.

Competing commitments. Competing commitments are value conflicts. For example, you might simultaneously hold both *innovation* and *risk avoidance* as values. One value may be at the forefront and the other unconscious, making it difficult to see and address this incongruity.

Impostor syndrome. An impostor is someone whose *identity* is greater than their capabilities. They're pretending to be better than they are. Impostor syndrome is when your *capability* is greater than your identity; in other words, you don't know how good you are. This is a very common syndrome, especially among entrepreneurs—and most especially among women entrepreneurs.

If people tell you how good you are or you're meeting with

[LEVELS OF CREATION]

success in the world, believe it. Own it. Make it part of your identity. You'll be surprised how you act differently and produce different results when you integrate your capabilities into your identity.

THE FUTUROSITY CONTINUUM

Moving from where you are now to the vision you want to create will require you to confront many choices. You'll have to choose between countless options, bifurcation points where your decisions will either take you closer to your vision or lead you down dead-ends.

Every choice you make puts you in a different relationship to time. Are you being led by the past or the future? Are you reacting to external forces or intentionally shaping the future you envision? You're constantly locating yourself along a continuum, with the past tugging at one end and the future pulling you from the other.

You create your future by making decisions and taking action. But how do you know which actions to take?

The *Futurosity Continuum* is a simple model to help you understand how you're allocating your time, energy, and resources. Knowing where you fall on this continuum can help you understand why you're not producing the results you want and how you can be more creative about your future.

Here's the Futurosity Continuum:

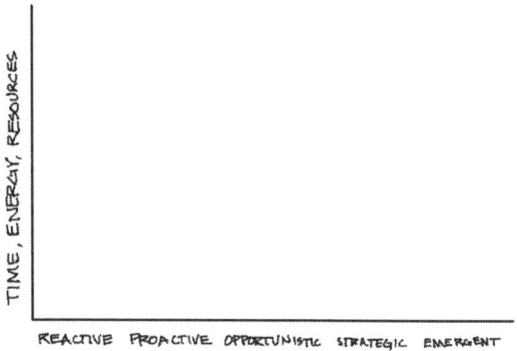

The y-axis of the continuum represents time, energy, and resources. The x-axis runs from reactive to proactive, opportunistic, strategic, and emergent. Each of these stances represents an orientation toward time, either compelling you to fix the past or pulling you to create the future.

REACTIVE

When you're in a reactive stance, you're responding to situations outside yourself. You're putting out fires. You're on the defense, responding to something that's already happened and solving past problems instead of creating future possibilities.

If you're solving the same problems over and over again, you can do a postmortem or retrospective to learn what went wrong and take measures to prevent the same issues from happening again.

[THE FUTUROSITY CONTINUUM]

PROACTIVE

When you're proactive, you're beginning to orient yourself toward the future instead of the past. You're not yet creating what you want; you're just preparing to get ahead of problems that might happen. You can do a *premortem*. Instead of reacting, you're looking for problems before they occur and taking steps to prevent them.

OPPORTUNISTIC

In an opportunistic stance, you're creating and taking advantage of opportunities that come your way. The more you put yourself out there, the more opportunities you'll create, and it will be tempting to take each one, even if they won't get you to B. At its best, being opportunistic can help you if you're on a quest and don't know exactly where you want to go. At its worst, opportunism becomes shiny object syndrome; you're just being distracted from what you really want.

STRATEGIC

You're being strategic when you're *intentionally* creating a future of your choosing. You're taking deliberate action to move toward your vision. You're constantly calibrating and adjusting to optimize for your vision, or an outcome even better than you imagined when you set out:—B-prime.

EMERGENT

If you're on a path, being strategic may be enough. You're clear about what you're trying to create, and you're intentional about taking the actions you know will produce your B.

But you're not on a path; you're on a quest. You're not creating from the past. Even if you're being intentional, you don't know how to create B-prime. You conduct experiments, try different things, and then *notice* how the universe responds.

Being strategic means being as clear as you can be and asking for what you want. It's a *monologue*.

Being emergent is asking what's possible and being in conversation with the universe. You try something, listen for a response, make adjustments, then try something else. It's a *dialogue*.

If you understand the Futurosity Continuum, you can plot how you spend your time, energy, and resources. For most people (and most leaders and organizations), the continuum graph looks like this:

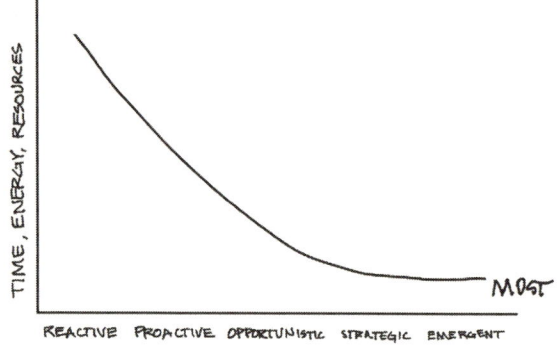

[THE FUTUROSITY CONTINUUM]

Things are a little different at a startup. A startup hasn't been around very long and may have fewer problems to solve and fewer challenges to react to. Compared to established companies, more of its time is spent being proactive (trying to anticipate customer needs) and opportunistic (trying different things to create many opportunities).

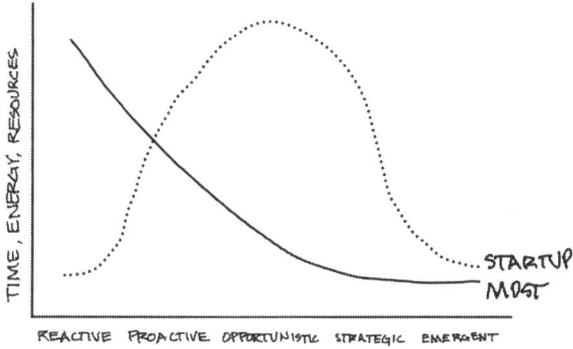

Ideally, the Futurosity Continuum looks like this:

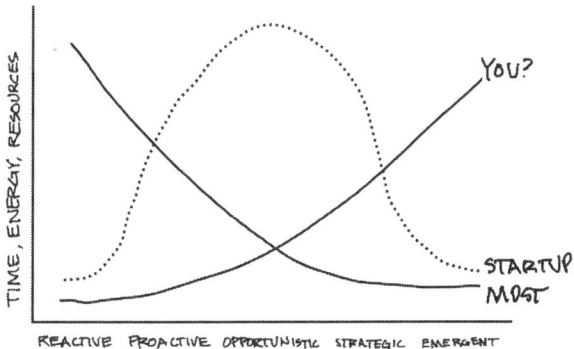

You'll always spend some of your time being reactive—you can't foresee everything. By definition, when you're reacting to something, you're reacting because something happened that wasn't in your control.

You can use the Futurosity Continuum like a compass.

With every choice you consider, ask yourself, "Am I being reactive? Am I being proactive? Is this an opportunity that's likely to move me closer to my vision, or is it a shiny object? Is this a strategic decision that will take me closer to my aim? Am I being emergent and paying close attention to the results I'm creating?"

The biggest trap is getting sidetracked by an opportunity that leads nowhere. Being emergent requires focus.

Are you being opportunistic or emergent?

Here's how you'll know:

Have a clear vision. You must have a clear picture of what you're trying to create. If you don't, you're not on a quest. You're drifting.

Pay attention to the results you get. Don't stubbornly persist if things don't work out as you expected. Pay attention and see what you can learn. What is the universe trying to tell you?

Know what you're saying NO to. It's helpful to know what you're creating and what you're actively *not* creating. It's addition by subtraction. Very often, the most strategic thing is subtracting or stopping an action altogether. Memorize these words from Steve Jobs: "People think focus means saying 'yes' to the thing you've got to focus on. But that's not what it means at all. It means saying 'no' to the hundred other good ideas that there are."

Know your values—and your essence. When deciding what to

do, make sure your actions align with your values and your essence.

<u>*Ask the essential question*</u>. If you have any doubts, ask yourself, <u>*If I choose this, who will I become?*</u>

OPTIMIZE FOR SERENDIPITY

How did you meet your spouse, significant other, lover, or friend?

Chance encounter? A random event? Did you meet at a bus stop? On an airplane? In line at the bakery?

Were you actively looking? Going to events, Meetups, and watering spots, or swiping left and right?

Did someone introduce you? A friend playing matchmaker? A blind or not-so-blind date?

Were you pursuing your life, being adventurous, not looking for anything in particular, but holding open the possibility that you might meet someone?

You most likely met your match in one of the four ways above.

It may have been *pure chance*. You were walking down the street, bumped into someone, looked up, the heavens opened, and there stood your soul mate. Lucky you (if serendipity is luck, then chance is *dumb* luck).

Maybe you made your luck through *curiosity* and *experimentation*. You went to social events or suffered through a queue of OkCupid, Bumble, or MeetMindful dates, intentionally

[COACHING FROM ESSENCE]

creating as many encounters as possible. (This is how I met my beloved.)

If your roommate's sister's girlfriend fixed you up with someone, you found your beloved through *making connections*.

If you were going to places you were interested in without any particular intention of finding someone, but you went with an open heart and mind, you were *wandering and wondering*.

We don't just meet people through serendipity. We also meet *ideas* through serendipity.

Splenda was invented when a scientist, told to "test" a new compound, heard "taste" instead and discovered that it was extremely sweet.

The Post-it Note was invented by a scientist trying to invent a superstrong adhesive. Experimenting in his lab, he found a super weak one instead. The Post-it Note languished in the lab for about six years. It was a solution in the search of a different problem. In other words, *it was a failure*. Until . . . a colleague, wandering and wondering in church one day, noticed his bookmark kept falling out of his hymn book. Problem of finding a problem—solved.

Keep this in mind as you come up with ideas for yourself or your clients. Maybe your "failures" are the solution to a different problem.

Something unique just happened. A miracle! A one in a million chance. How did it happen?

There's a law that explains it. It's Littlewood's law of miracles, named after Cambridge University Professor John Edensor Littlewood.

Littlewood calculated that an "event" occurs about once every second. He conservatively estimated that we're alert for

[OPTIMIZE FOR SERENDIPITY]

about eight hours a day. In thirty-five days, we experience about one million events. Every thirty-five days, something happens that has only a one in a million chance of happening. In other words, *a miracle*.

He didn't set out to prove the existence of miracles. He wanted to prove that extraordinary events are commonplace because so many events occur. Life is, to a greater degree than we might like to admit, a numbers game.

Your clients can follow their known path—or they can optimize for serendipity by using one of the methods outlined above: pure chance, curiosity and experimentation, making connections, or wandering and wondering. Whatever their strategy, they can improve their chances of creating something better than they can imagine by simply going on a quest, thereby increasing the number of events and, consequently, increasing the number of possible miracles.

If you do the work, success is assured but not predictable. You *will* succeed; it's just impossible to say precisely how or when. That's not metaphysics. It's statistics.

Thanks, John.

HOW TO KNOCK OVER THE EMPIRE STATE BUILDING

You can knock over the Empire State Building with twenty-nine dominos. Each domino knocks over the next domino, which is about one-and-a-half times its mass. The last domino is as tall as the Empire State Building.

Here's the real question: *How big does the first domino have to be?*

About the size of a breath mint!

What does this mean for you?

Most people get clear on their B, their Empire State Building, and they get excited and try to knock over the tenth domino. They push, and they push, and they can't knock it over, and they say to themselves, "I was right all along. It's not possible to have what I want. It's not possible to create a form that matches my essence."

And they give up.

Instead, <u>if you start with the biggest, smallest step you can take, the step you know you can do and not fail</u>, you will soon create so much momentum that you're knocking over the tenth domino with ease.

The critical thing to understand is that it must be the

[COACHING FROM ESSENCE]

BIGGEST smallest step you can take. It has to be big enough that it matters—it will move you closer to your aim—and small enough that success is assured.

If you're trying to build your coaching practice, that step might be going to a networking event. It's big enough—it has the potential to lead to some prospects—but it's also small enough (if you go, you've already succeeded in getting out of the house and going, and you've likely learned something as well).

String enough of those small dominos together, and suddenly you're knocking over some meaningful stuff.

BEGIN BEFORE YOU'RE READY

You think you're not ready, but you are.

Maybe you're new to coaching, and you're wondering if you need to be certified or go back to school. Maybe you already have a coaching practice and want to do more profound work or raise your fees.

You tell yourself you'll start coaching when you're certified or graduate from a coaching program. You'll begin to work differently after you've read a few more books, or you'll raise your fees when your practice is finally full and you see clients every day of the week.

You're not the only one.

Your clients aren't ready. They're not ready to quit the passionless job that's going nowhere with the boss they hate. They're not ready to launch their startup. They have a brilliant idea but not the faintest idea of how to begin. Maybe Stanford has an online course.

You'll never be ready.

They'll never be ready.

But it's too late for ready. Wherever you think you're going,

[COACHING FROM ESSENCE]

you've been on this journey your whole life. You've already begun.
   Forget ready.
   Begin before you're ready.
   Time to knock over your next domino.

III

FORM AND ESSENCE

*Everyone is a genius.
But if you judge a fish by its ability to climb a tree,
it will live its whole life believing
that it is stupid.*
—Albert Einstein (or maybe not)

FORM AND ESSENCE

WE LIVE IN a world of form.

A form is a *shape, frame, condition, agreement, etc.*

Everything you see, hear, touch—everything you experience with your senses—is a form.

Thoughts are forms, too.

Your beliefs. Your identity. Your roles. All forms.

Forms are *not* essence.

Many forms are social conveniences.

I'm Robert Ellis. I'm an executive coach. I'm married.

Those are all forms. They make life easy. Forms dispel mysteries. We attach meaning to forms and pretend that we understand them. You can imagine that you know something about me. Robert Ellis, executive coach, married.

To be alive is to be entangled, ensnared, engulfed in forms. We cling to forms as if they are life rafts. They save us from drowning in mystery and possibilities. But they also limit us.

The *aim* of Coaching From Essence is to decouple people from their attachment to forms, to empower them to navigate forms, and, ultimately, to create forms that are congruent with their essence.

[COACHING FROM ESSENCE]

Everyone has an essence.

(Organizations do, too.)

The *essence* of Coaching From Essence is the conviction that everyone has a natural way of being in the world that adds value without any thought or effort on their part.

[handwritten annotations: soulful, exploring new territory, connection, freedom, empathy, growing, nature]

WHAT ESSENCE IS

Natural way of being means innate, integral. Essence is not something you learn; it's something you *are*. You can get better at it, but you already *are* it.

Adds value means contribution, gift, service. Essence is always positive.

Essence is so natural and so effortless that it is often hidden from the person; it's overlooked, under-appreciated, taken for granted. It is deep and reliable, a source of innate strength and power.

Your essence is *alive*.

Essence is palpable but elusive. It is a mistake to cling too tightly to any particular expression of your essence. You will think you understand it, and then you'll realize you don't.

Essence is like love. You have a relationship with essence that deepens over time. Essence will unfold.

Keep it simple.

Keep it beautiful and mysterious.

WHAT ESSENCE IS NOT

Essence is not *purpose*. Purpose is about motivation and intention. I don't believe we are born with one purpose. We can

[56]

[FORM AND ESSENCE]

have multiple purposes, and we may be motivated to do something that may or may not have anything to do with our essence (but we'll be happier if we choose a purpose that's congruent with our essence).

Essence is not *passion*. Passion is love, enthusiasm, or obsession for something. You may not be passionate about your essence. It's likely that you're *not* particularly passionate about your essence simply because it comes so naturally to you. You're likely to take it for granted. You may become passionate about a *form* that allows you to express your essence.

Coaching is one of my passions, but it's not my essence. It's a form that *matches* my essence.

Essence is not the same as *personality*. You might think of it as a subset of personality. Personality refers to individual differences in characteristic patterns of thinking, feeling and behaving. But many of those differences are learned, not innate.

Essence is not the same as your values or *priorities*. Your priorities may be out of alignment with your essence.

I'm against trying to reduce essence to an *essence statement*, an exact definition. That's not the purpose of essence. I want the concept of essence to remain a bit mysterious because then it's a love relationship, something that can grow, that can surprise us.

WHAT IS COACHING FROM ESSENCE?

Coaching From Essence is a form. It's an *expression of my* essence (but it's not my essence).

There *is* an essence to Coaching From Essence that is not about its form. There is something here that is not about the language or the models or the tools.

[COACHING FROM ESSENCE]

You are free to play with this form, and to take as much of the essence as you can and make it yours, but it's not your essence. You have your own beautiful essence to bring to the world. Bring it.

FIND YOUR ESSENCE

In the spring of 2016, I attended Hive—The Global Community for Leaders and Entrepreneurs. One focus of the workshop was helping participants clarify their purpose. The hundred-plus attendees were divided into smaller groups, which met several times during the program to process what we were learning and to support each other.

On the last evening of the program, one of the women in my group sighed with frustration. The graduation ceremony would take place the following evening, with all participants sitting in an open circle. Each person would have the opportunity to step into that vast empty space, face their fellow humans, and proclaim why they were alive.

Flipping through her workbook, she struggled to distill all the exercises into a purpose statement she could write on our final one-page worksheet.

She was distraught. She'd done all the exercises, but somehow it didn't add up.

I was having my own challenges, so I was happy to take a break from my agonizing self-reflection to answer her pleas for help. I sat next to her and asked her to walk me through her thoughts. She began to list all of the things she had done in her life, an eclectic laundry list of seemingly unrelated experiences—a fascinating life composed of incredible parts but missing a whole.

I asked her two simple questions: "What is the thread that runs through all of the things you have ever done? When you were being your best self, who were you being?" [handwritten annotations: Related, Present, Enthusiastic, Connected]

She began poring through her notes again, like an accountant looking for that missing penny.

I took my seat on the other side of the table. I wish I could say that I figured out my purpose that weekend, that it all became clear to me, but it didn't. The closest thing I could come up with was, *I help purpose-driven leaders dream bigger, act bolder, and do the impossible.* It would have looked good on a business card, but it wasn't my purpose, and it wasn't my essence.

That came sometime later.

The woman in the workshop balanced her books. I don't remember her purpose, but it resonated with her.

After the program, I asked myself the same two questions. I looked at my checkered past, my own laundry list of seemingly unrelated experiences across the decades—talent manager, therapist, personal growth workshop leader, futures broker, car salesman (I never sold *used* cars), freelance writer for *Macworld*, acupuncturist (was licensed but never practiced), executive coach (I'm leaving out a lot here to spare you the details)—and I found the thread that ran through them all, a little strand of DNA.

What was it that I could not stop doing? I couldn't stop trying to help people get what they wanted, to create the future they wanted. I helped them see themselves as rock stars, or happy in their relationships, or rich, or joyfully cruising down the highway, or a power user, or healed, or—the wild card—

whatever it was they wanted to create for themselves or their organization.

I can't help but do that. Everywhere I go, everyone I meet, once we're past the pleasantries, I will be listening for their longing and inviting them to dream with me.

I sometimes say, as a shorthand, *my essence is helping people create the future.*

But that's not my essence. You could easily call that a purpose, although it's not really a purpose, either. It's just the way that I express something about who I am naturally.

There's also the *way* that I help people create the future. I don't even know how I do that. I know something about it—the ideas and models I use—and that's what I'm sharing with you here.

But there's also the way I show up in my essence.

It's helpful when clients give me feedback about how they experience me, that my energy is sometimes piercing, for example. I do think that's part of my essence. I have a way of taking complex ideas, really focusing them, distilling things down, and turning them into something simple.

Those are clues to my essence.

But they are not my *essence*.

I am still learning about my essence.

IS THERE AN ESSENCE INSTRUMENT?

People love personality models and instruments. Wouldn't it be fantastic if you could answer a simple questionnaire and know your essence?

Myers-Briggs, CliftonStrengths, Strengths Profile. Any number of instruments will tell you something about your personality and strengths, and because essence is a subset of personality, these insights may contain clues to your essence. But they will not tell you your essence.

All of these instruments are trying to answer the question, *What does the inside of a person look like?*

It's like asking, *What does the inside of an apple look like?*

It depends very much on how you cut the apple.

Cut it vertically, and it looks one way. Cut it horizontally, and it looks another way.

I rarely use these instruments with clients (though I have used them, or similar models, in the past). If you do use these tools with your clients, I recommend using more than one to at least give your clients a more three-dimensional view of themselves.

HOW TO FIND YOUR ESSENCE

I want you to engage your essence in a conversation and deepen your relationship with essence over time. There is no path to your essence.

Finding your essence is a quest.

I know that isn't a very satisfying answer, so I'll give you a few suggestions for self-reflection and for working with your clients.

FIND THE THREAD

As I asked the woman at the workshop, ask yourself, "What is the thread that runs through all the things I have ever done? When I was being my best self, who was I being?"

Regardless of the form it took, what were you doing in every

[FIND YOUR ESSENCE]

job you've ever had? What was the essence of what you were doing? For example, if all of your jobs involved talking to people, your essence may have something to do with communication. Maybe you're a connector.

There may be a few outliers, but you'll find that there was something always looking for expression.

ASK YOUR FRIENDS (AND CLIENTS)

Everyone you know, especially those close to you and everyone you've ever worked with, are excellent sources of information about your essence. They know better than you do how you show up and who you are at your best (and your worst).

What do your friends come to you for? listen, wisdom, different perspectives

What problems do they bring? What do they rely on you for?

Ask them, "If I weren't in your life, what would you miss? How am I different from the other people you know? When you think of me, what comes immediately to mind? Who am I at my best?"

Make up your own questions. Become curious about their experience with you. They will have insights for you.

Finding your essence is like the blind men and the elephant. One blind man grabs the leg and thinks it's a tree. Another grabs the trunk and thinks it's a rope. No one has the whole understanding of who you are. Everyone may have a different *sense* of your *essence*. Other people are often a valuable source of information about your essence, but it's easy for them to confuse essence with personality or skills. Take the information as clues, not truth.

Only you can say what your essence truly is.

[COACHING FROM ESSENCE]

GO BACK. WAY BACK.

Clues to your essence were there very early in your life, possibly from birth.

When you're looking for the thread that makes sense of your life, don't stop at the onset of adulthood. Don't limit yourself to professional experiences.

Go back. Way back.

What are some of your earliest memories?

What were you like as a kid? (If you can't remember, ask your parents or siblings.)

Pull out old photos. *Who do you see behind your child eyes?*

We learn how to distance ourselves from our essence early in life. It's usually a painful process.

When you were a kid, *what made you cry?* ET

What makes you cry now?

BECOME CURIOUS AND CONDUCT EXPERIMENTS

Once you have some clues to your essence—and they are always there, always listen for them in yourself and your clients—you can turn those clues into experiments. You go on a quest to test your ideas. You take a few steps down multiple paths, craft miniature forms to see what it feels like.

If you think your essence has something to do with how you communicate, you might start by writing. Go on a quest to find your voice and the words you've been carrying that need to be said.

If you think your essence has something to do with how you connect people with others, or create experiences, listen, hold space, or heal—find a form to pour some of that connection or experience or listening or space-holding or healing into. See what emerges and hold the results lightly.

TAKE GOOD NOTES

Create a document, take out a piece of paper, or, better yet, open your journal. Start keeping an inventory of everything you're learning about your essence.

Draw two lines to divide the page into three columns.

Label the first column, **IS**. Under this column, list all of the clues you're gathering about your essence that resonate with you.

The second column, label **IS NOT**. List all the things you know your essence isn't, all the clues or forms that don't resonate.

Label the third column, **IS IT?** Here, you can list all of your questions. They may be about essence or forms that you think may resonate with your essence, but you're not sure yet. Turn these questions into Quest(ions). Conduct experiments.

You will learn the most about your essence by allowing it to express itself in the world. That's what your essence wants. If you're expressing your essence, it will make you happier. If you are trying to express your essence and feel no satisfaction, you have either misunderstood the conversation you're having with your essence or miscalculated the form your essence is longing for.

Keep learning.

THE ESSENTIAL CHOICE

LIFE PRESENTS US with a clear and compelling choice about how to live.

On one side is what I call the hidden curriculum. This curriculum includes everything we've been taught about how to win in life: s*elf-interest, status-seeking, scarcity, and survival.*

The rules of following this curriculum are simple:

–I come first. *What can I get?*
–Look good at all costs.
–There's not enough. (I'm not enough.)
–Play it safe. (Hide your pain. Never confront the Love threshold.)

We cling to this game even though it has never, and will never, make us happy.

There's another more natural and fulfilling way to show up for your life: *live from essence, abundance, service, and trust.*

The rules for this way of living are also simple:

[COACHING FROM ESSENCE]

—What's good for you is good for me. *What can I give?*
—I'm okay (even if I don't look good).
—There's more than enough. The more I give, the more I have. (I'm enough.)
—It's okay. *Really.* (The universe will support me in expressing my essence in this world.)

What I know in my bones—from my personal work and my work with clients—is that coming from essence, abundance, service, and trust is the key to happiness and success.

If only it were easy.

Most of us are more afraid of living from essence, abundance, service, and trust than from self-interest, status-seeking, scarcity, and survival. We have been taught from a very early age that self-interest is the key to survival and, paradoxically, to winning love.

You have to start choosing your essence every day.

You have to trust that the world will support you if you do. If you can't take that leap of faith and prove to yourself that you can be supported for being your best self, you will never be able to convince your clients to do so, either.

Your essence is calling you. It's what you're longing for.

It's calling your clients, too.

That's the journey they really want to make if you can help them believe it's possible.

It is.

THE ESSENCE QUESTIONS

Whenever I have to make an important decision, I ask myself three questions. I call them *The Essence Questions* because I designed them to keep me in alignment with my essence.

When I'm coaching clients, and we're thinking together about the possible solutions to a problem, or we're mulling over a decision, I explore these same three questions.

Here are the three Essence Questions:

1. Will this create a life you love?
2. Will this be of true service, in alignment with your essence?
3. Who will you become?

WILL THIS CREATE A LIFE YOU LOVE?

To answer this question, you need to know what it would look like to have a life you love. You need to know something about your *values*.

Some coaches work with various values exercises to help their clients get at this, and those exercises can be useful. I prefer to listen for the values hidden in the stories clients tell.

Become curious. Listen to what your client loves.

Listen to what you love.

WILL THIS BE OF TRUE SERVICE, IN ALIGNMENT WITH YOUR ESSENCE?

Choosing a life you love is an act of self-care. But if you *only* choose what is good for you, you would be coming *only* from self-interest.

Essence wants to be of service. It's our natural way of adding value without any thought or effort on our part.

When you're choosing between life paths, you want to choose a life you love that also creates the best opportunity for you to serve in the way that is most congruent with your essence.

Listen for how your client naturally adds value. Essence is not *form*. Don't become too attached to form, and don't let your client become too attached to form. The form doesn't matter as long as it provides an opportunity for you to express more and more of your best self—your essence—and you will like who you become.

WHO WILL YOU BECOME?

After we've narrowed the options down to something of service that the client would love doing, I ask them, "If you go on this journey, who will you become?"

When you go on a journey, you not only get something—B

[THE ESSENCE QUESTIONS]

or B-prime or B-sub—you become someone. You might become a martyr. You might become a tyrant.

The world has enough martyrs and tyrants.
Don't let your clients become martyrs or tyrants.
Don't become a martyr or tyrant.
Become your best self.

WHAT YOU WERE BORN TO DO

Everyone was *born* to do something beautiful.

Paul Potts was a manager at Carphone Warehouse, selling mobile phones, but his essence was singing—opera.

In 2007, he won the first series of *Britain's Got Talent*. He went on to record an album that topped sales charts in thirteen countries. When I first saw the video of his winning performance of "Nessun Dorma," an aria from Puccini's opera *Turandot* (I know nothing about opera and am not a fan)—I wept.

Most of us do something we were not born to do—our version of selling mobile phones (there's nothing wrong with selling mobile phones if that's what you're born to do).

What you were born to do is to live the life that wants to be lived through you, *to give full expression to your essence*.

When someone like Paul Potts comes to you for coaching, *see the opera singer in them*, not the mobile phone salesperson. Help them see it—and believe it—too.

Coaching From Essence means doing the work you were born to do, bringing more and more of your essence into form.

And it means helping our clients do the same.

IV

THE RED PAPERCLIP

*A wise person should have money in their head,
but not in their heart.*
—Jonathan Swift

THE RED PAPERCLIP

Remember, you can knock over the Empire State Building with twenty-nine dominos, and the first one doesn't need to be any bigger than a breath mint.

Similarly, you can start with a red paperclip and, after a series of favorable trades, end up with a house.

Kyle MacDonald wrote the book on how to do just that—*One Red Paperclip*. He traded the paperclip for a fish-shaped pen, then a hand-sculpted doorknob, and so on. His last trade was for a two-story farmhouse in Kipling, Saskatchewan.

How many trades do you think it took for him to go from red paperclip to farmhouse?

When you're starting your coaching practice, it isn't worth very much. You may be coaching pro bono for quite some time. The first year I started coaching from my essence, most of my clients were pro bono or low bono (they paid a negotiated reduced fee).

I grew my coaching and leadership training practice a little over fourfold in three years. How do you move from coaching pro bono to creating a coaching practice worth multiple six figures?

[COACHING FROM ESSENCE]

I did it by trading up a red paperclip. The paperclip was my pro bono coaching. Then I coached someone for $250 per month and kept increasing my fees until I landed my first CEO client, who paid $10k per month (he paid $30k in advance for three months, no refunds).

It's easier to build your practice by attracting clients who have more at stake and are more capable of paying higher fees than by trying to raise your rates on existing clients.

You don't want to raise your fees; *you want to raise your clients*.

I only raise my fee if the client's financial situation has changed since we began coaching (particularly if their financial situation has changed as a direct result of coaching) or if I'm doing more work for them (for example, if I'm working with the CEO, and they decide they want me to coach members of the leadership team).

If you are just beginning to build your practice, the most important thing is to create a full practice, even if all your clients are pro bono. *Then trade them up.*

As you become more confident in your skills and your practice grows by referral, you can level up your practice, work with higher-level executives, and charge higher fees (you don't have to, of course, this isn't all about making money).

Keep trading up. Don't worry about the money. If you do the work, you will succeed. I can't tell you when or how, but success is assured. Recall Littlewood's law of miracles. It's not metaphysics; it's statistics.

It took only fourteen trades to go from a red paperclip to a two-story farmhouse.

But you have to start with that red paperclip. You have to start with your first client.

Here's how to create clients.

CREATE CLIENTS YOU LOVE

I HAVE AN incredible coaching practice full of clients I love.

It wasn't always that way.

A few years ago, I accepted every client who came my way, whether or not they were a good fit. It wasn't very satisfying.

Now my practice is full, I'm doing more powerful work than ever (client feedback), and I love—*love*—my clients.

What changed?

I completely reinvented the way I work as a coach.

I used to hide behind professional distance. I was half-hearted. I didn't show up fully.

One of my intentions when I reinvented myself, and the way I work, was that I wanted to be *wholehearted*. I didn't want to hide behind a professional persona. I didn't want to maintain a professional distance. I wanted to be open to having a deeper, more personal connection with the people I work with.

Now, I invite people into a different conversation, a different relationship. I do it intentionally, make clear agreements, and commit to creating a bigger space where more—much more—can be included in the conversation.

[COACHING FROM ESSENCE]

To attract the people you want and filter out the people you don't want, you need to be clear about who you want to work with.

When I started coaching, I just wanted to make a lot of money. I attracted clients, but I didn't particularly love working with some of them. I had no idea who my ideal client was.

Knowing your ideal client can help you identify the people you will resonate with and will truly be able to serve. They're a good match for what you, in your essence, offer. They give you an opportunity to learn and grow.

Most of my clients are entrepreneurs, CEOs, or coaches who work with entrepreneurs and CEOs. But my ideal client isn't a title, a demographic, or someone who meets some particular financial criteria. It took me a long time to understand who my ideal client was.

A few years ago, when I wasn't as happy as I am now with my coaching practice, I fell in love with a client. Actually, I fell in love with the entire executive team.

I had so much fun working with them. I would come home energized. The work was challenging—edgework that took me out of my comfort zone. It was intellectually stimulating. Many on the team were trying to accomplish something they had never done before. There was a lot at stake (millions of dollars), and the team was committed to succeeding together. Everyone on the team had the attitude of a learner. They showed up in a supportive way for each other.

I knew there was something different about working with them. I started to journal about my experience. I made lists. What qualities of these people made it so enjoyable and satisfying to work with them? What was it about the work that made it so fulfilling for me?

It took more than a year for things to crystalize. I now

know—very clearly—who my ideal client is. When I do a dream session with someone, if they are interested in creating a coaching relationship, I let them know I have very specific criteria for who I work with. I tell them I'll walk them through the criteria, and they can tell me whether or not they feel we're a good fit.

First, there has to be a lot at stake. What we're working on has to be so important that failure is not an option. It has to be so aspirational that the client knows they will have to undergo a personal transformation to achieve it.

Second, the quest has to be a net positive. I don't work with clients I feel are making the world worse. Most of my clients are impact entrepreneurs or engaged in projects that will have some positive impact on the world.

Third, they have to be coachable. How open are they to other points of view? How willing are they to take feedback? I will test them, asking them what I call *a disturbing question*, or a *provocation*, in the first session to see if they will engage with me.

Fourth, they have to be all in. That means three things. They are willing to put everything on the table (one of my core beliefs, which I discuss with the client in the first session, is that you can't separate who you are professionally from who you are personally). They have to make a real commitment (I don't work with anyone for less than three months, and they pay in advance). And the fee can't be an issue (I charge CEOs $10k per month). If it is, I go back to the first criteria and ask, "Is this important enough to you that you are willing to make a meaningful investment in yourself?"

Finally, *I have to like them.* I think they will be fun to work with, they have a sense of humor, I might learn something. If we're not going to enjoy working together, we're not a good fit.

I recommend you do this exercise yourself. Who is *your* ideal client?

Your criteria should be different from mine. Think of all the clients you've worked with. Some you loved, some you liked, some you tolerated, some you couldn't wait for the engagement to be over. What did the clients you love have in common? Write it down. Share your criteria with your prospective clients.

When I started sharing my criteria with prospective clients at the end of my dream sessions, I noticed something fascinating. Many began trying to persuade me that they fit the criteria. "This means a lot to me," they'd say, "I *think* I'm coachable. I hope you like me."

They enrolled themselves.

And why wouldn't they? If it wasn't true that they fit the criteria, they wanted it to be true. They wanted to be creating things that mattered, that had a positive impact. They wanted to be coachable. They wanted to be more committed in their lives. They wanted to have more fun.

Another fascinating thing happened after I got crystal clear about who my ideal client was.

They began to show up.

SHOW, DON'T TELL

Show, don't tell. Coach, don't sell.

You will not get coaching clients by telling them what you do or what they will get by working with you. You only get coaching clients by coaching them.

Whenever you meet someone who might be a potential client, someone you might be able to serve, be open to having a conversation with the intention of being helpful.

Do your best to give them something of value.

Always ask for permission first. If you meet someone and get into a conversation that feels like a coaching conversation, say, "Listen, I have some thoughts about that. Would you be interested in some observations?" Or, "Would it be okay if I gave you a different way to think about that?"

If you coach before you get permission, it will sound like you're reprimanding or judging the person.

Always ask.

I once had a coaching session with a woman in her office at one of the largest high-tech companies in Silicon Valley. While I was there, she said, "I was telling a friend about you, and she's

[COACHING FROM ESSENCE]

here from New York. Can I introduce you? I'd love for you to meet each other."

I said, "Sure."

She finds the woman and introduces us, and we start talking. The woman tells me she's thinking about making a career change and looking for someone to help her figure out how to position herself to get a better job. She asks me about coaching. She wants to know how it works.

Instead of telling her about coaching, I say, "Would you be open to doing some work now?"

"What do you mean? Like right now?"

"Yeah," I say. "We have a few minutes. Would you like to do some coaching right now?"

"Okay," she says.

So I started coaching. I coached her for literally five minutes.

She got so excited that she started asking me about the process of working with me. "How much does it cost?"

I told her what I always tell people. "Obviously, this is a longer conversation. Here's what I'm willing to do. Let's put something on the calendar right now. Let's block out two hours so we can have a meaningful conversation. I'll coach you, and then we'll both know whether we're a good fit. If we are, we can talk about what it would look like to work together."

I asked for permission before coaching, but I didn't try to tell her what coaching was about or what it would do for her. I didn't try to sell her anything (if I sell anything to anybody, I sell people on themselves). I created value for her in the moment. Because of that value, she had the experience that something else might be possible for her if she worked with me.

She "sold" herself.

DREAM TOGETHER

Many coaches think of the first session as a "teaser" session, "fit conversation," "needs assessment," or "discovery" session. I don't think of it that way.

It's important to understand what your goals are for the first session.

One goal is to establish rapport and build trust. + resonance

Before the coronavirus, I liked meeting clients in cafes (now I coach clients all over the world via Zoom). Why? What do people usually do when they meet people for coffee? They talk about personal things. I want them to feel comfortable talking to me about personal things—like their most authentic dreams. It's easier to create a personal relationship in a less formal space. Most of my clients are executives. *Not all life coaching is executive coaching, but all executive coaching is life coaching.*

The second goal is to *hear their story*. I'm listening for their Levels of Creation, especially their identity (their beliefs about themselves), their beliefs about what they're trying to create, and their values.

Third, and most importantly, I'm also *listening for their essence*, their way of being in the world that adds value without

[COACHING FROM ESSENCE]

any thought or effort. My role as their coach is to help them create a form in the world that's congruent with their essence so they can be more successful and fulfilled.

I'm not focused on their needs because I know those will change.

Our task is to be curious and help them look at their story and then reflect it back to them. When they share a limiting belief, point it out. "You know, that's a belief. Is that really true?" When they share a value (and they're not going to say, "I value creativity," they're going to say something like, "I wish I were doing work that wasn't so routine"), you can reflect, "Sounds like one of your values is creativity. Are you working toward something that allows you to express your creativity?"

You're listening to their story, but you're not focused on the content. You're listening for what's underneath and reflecting that back.

Giving them plenty of time to tell their story does a couple of things.

It helps them feel seen and heard, which is incredibly important because, for many people, that's half the value of coaching. There may be no other relationship in their life where they feel seen and heard the way you see and hear them. Being seen and heard is incredibly powerful for creating something. When people feel seen and heard for who they are and what they want, it's empowering.

Encourage them to tell their story by being more curious, asking open-ended questions, and getting them to open up. Some coaches think it's not a good idea to let people go on and on about their stories, but it's one of the reasons I do two-hour sessions. Letting people tell their stories and reveal themselves can be incredibly rich.

I'm not listening to how they're defining a problem. I'm

[DREAM TOGETHER]

listening to what's speaking through their words. And I'm reflecting that underlying essence back to them, and then I'm saying, "Great! So what is it you're trying to create? Let's dream together. If we were to work together, what would you want to create?"

They will almost always tell you a crippled version of their true dream, a bonsai dream, or a dream they stole from someone else. Challenge that. Break apart their bonsai dream, crack their glass bottle, and get them to dream a dream as true, authentic, and resonant as they can.

If you do nothing else in the dream session, helping them articulate a true dream is powerful. That's why I have prospective clients talk about dreams instead of needs. Needs are based on the past. You don't want to help them create something based on their past. You want to help them create from a future of unlimited possibilities.

If you can help them dream a true dream, it's a good reason for them to work with you. If they're creating something they already know how to create, if they want to create a bonsai dream, they probably don't need you. If they're pursuing a goal they already know they can create, they don't need a coach. Your job is to help them dream something so aspirational that they say, "Wow, you know, that's what I really want, and I recognize that's not possible for me right now. Not only would I have to do a lot of things, but I would have to change to create that."

When they realize that creating their true dream is something they've never done before, something that will require a personal transformation, they will understand why they want a coach. And if you've helped them realize that, they'll know why they want *you to* be their coach.

CREATE A COACHING ALLIANCE

How do you turn a dream session into a coaching client?

First, coach your heart out. Do your best to change the person's life in an hour and a half, whether they become your client or not. If they don't become a client, they'll talk about you to someone, and that person may become a client (this has happened to me more than once). And even if they don't talk about you, you will have made a difference. It's *big heart practice*—you will have served out of an abundance of self and made a difference in someone's life, reinforcing your identity as a coach.

After about an hour and a half, the dream session will naturally begin to close. You summarize what you've accomplished and say something like this: "Let me check in with you. How was this for you?"

They will likely say something positive, if only to be polite.

Then ask, "Would you be interested in having another coaching conversation?" This is your transition into your enrollment conversation.

Rarely, if ever, will they say no. They might say, "I think I'm

[COACHING FROM ESSENCE]

good. You've given me a lot to think about. I need some time to absorb all of it." And that's fine. Good work.

They may respond by saying, "Well, how does that work?" Or, "Yeah, I'd love to have another conversation."

Here's what I say then: "Great! So it seems like I'm a good fit for you. Let's see if you're a fit for me. I h<u>ave very specific</u> crit<u>eria for who I work with.</u> Here they are: I only coach people working on something where there's a lot at stake—personally, professionally, or financially. Second, the outcome has to be a net positive. I don't work with people who are making the world worse. Most of my clients are impact entrepreneurs working in one way or another to make the world a better place. Third, you have to be coachable. You're not always going to agree with me, but <u>you have to be open.</u> You have to be willing to try <u>things on</u> and have your <u>thinking</u> challenged. Fourth, you have to be all in. That means two things: I'm a big believer that you can't separate who you are personally from who you are professionally, so everything is on the table. And the fee can't be an issue. If the fee is an issue, go back to number one. How important is this to you? Finally, I have to like you. I have to think it would be fun for us to work together, you have a sense of humor, I might learn something too."

When you're finished telling them your criteria for your ideal client, pause. Then ask them, "How does that fit for you?"

Your criteria won't be the same as mine, but if you're talking to people who might be a good fit, they'll likely respond to your criteria.

If they say it all sounds good, you can talk logistics. "Here's what it would look like for us to work together. Here's the typical cadence," and so on.

And then you can say, "L<u>et's talk about the fee." Don't wait</u> for the<u>m to as</u>k. If they ask too early in the conversation, tell

[CREATE A COACHING ALLIANCE]

them you're happy to discuss it later. "Let's get to know each other first."

When you talk about your fee, don't hesitate. Say whatever your fee is. Say it in a matter-of-fact tone, as if you were saying your name.

If I'm talking to the CEO of a well-funded company, I say, "The fee is $10,000 per month retainer. We meet twice a month for two hours, or weekly for an hour, but you have virtually unlimited access to me. You can call me or ping me anytime, within reason. I trust both of us to know what's reasonable. You're not on the clock. I'm here for you. I usually respond within twenty-four hours, rarely forty-eight hours if I'm traveling or at a client offsite. If you need to hop on a quick call, ping me first, and I'll call you back."

I have never had anyone take advantage of this, but leaders love to know they have virtually unlimited access to you. Less than half of my clients have contacted me for a coaching session outside our scheduled sessions.

I tell everyone my full fee, even if I know they will be a pro bono client. I want them to know the value of what I'm offering. If you know someone isn't in a position to pay your full fee, say something like this: "If you were the CEO of a well-funded company, my fee would be $10,000 a month. I know you're not in a position to pay that, so we need to agree on a fee representing a real *commitment* on your part and *fairness* to me."

And then you negotiate.

If you're beginning to build your practice and you're not comfortable charging for your coaching (why aren't you comfortable charging for your coaching?), you can say something like, "Listen, I'm just starting to do more coaching. I'd be willing to do three coaching sessions (or whatever number of sessions you're comfortable offering) with you gratis (don't say *free*). After that, if you're interested in continuing, we can talk about what would be an exchange of value that would respect both of us for the work that we're doing. Or maybe three sessions is all you'll need, and that would be fine too."

Don't make long-term commitments to your pro and low bono clients. Fill your practice as soon as you can, then *trade up your red paperclip*.

Never end the conversation on money. Always end the enrollment conversation by talking about *commitment*.

There are four commitments that I ask all of my clients to make:

– *Be all in.* We already talked about this when I presented my ideal client criteria to them.

– *They're responsible for the agenda.* They need to show up for our sessions knowing what they want from coaching. As we work together, I'll have ideas that might be helpful and bring those to the table, but I can't tell them where they want to go.

– *Keep all agreements.* If they say they will do something, I expect them to keep their word. A client will sometimes agree to take on homework. If they do, I trust that they will do it. One of the agreements I ask of all my clients is to send me their notes, insights, and actions within a couple of days of a session. Some of them won't agree to this, but if they do, I expect them to do it. For most of my clients, I create a Google Drive folder, and they keep their notes in a Google Doc or, if they take handwritten notes, they will often take pictures and upload their notes after our sessions.

– *Feedback and responsiveness.* A coaching relationship should be one relationship in your life where you never have to guess where you stand. We give each other feedback. I will ask the client for feedback at the beginning or end of almost every session, and I will be liberal with mine.

[CREATE A COACHING ALLIANCE]

Responsiveness is about avoiding stories. I commit to responding to my clients within twenty-four to forty-eight hours. We close the loop. For example, if someone sends me their notes, I always acknowledge them, whether or not I comment on them. I don't want a client wondering what I thought about their notes if they've shared something vulnerable, and I didn't respond.

These commitments are for the client, and I make the same commitments to them. If they don't keep them, I don't beat them up; I remind them of their commitment. I'm not an accountability partner; that's babysitting. If someone wants to work with me, they have to show up powerfully. And they do.

BOUNDARIES

For decades, I hid behind my professional persona, keeping a professional distance. Then I realized that doing so made me very unhappy. My work wasn't satisfying. It got in the way of deep work. People don't trust you if they don't know you. If you don't let them see you as a human being, it's tough for them to be open with you.

How do you balance being the coach and holding space for your clients while being a human being and showing up with some personal vulnerability? When is it okay to tell your story to the client? Aren't you in danger of stepping on therapy territory if you're diving too deep into the personal?

I share my personal stories with clients for a handful of reasons: to build rapport, to deepen our connection, to normalize something they may be struggling with, to provide examples that provoke thinking, show my humanity, and bring my whole heart to the conversation.

There is only one criterion for talking about yourself with a client: *Is this the most helpful thing I can say right now?*

The most important consideration is timing. I don't share until the client has told their story and they have felt heard and understood. Then I might say, "Listen, is it okay if I share something personal with you? I went through a similar challenge. And here's what I learned. I don't know if this is helpful to you. Let me share my experience, and you can see whether it's helpful for you to think about it that way."

That *doesn't* mean the coaching is about *me*. When I have a conversation with my clients, the focus is on them. I never tell my story with the intention of trying to tell the client what to do or for me to get some personal validation or support. If I have gone through something, and I have some experience that may be relevant, I may share it with a client. But I'm not asking them to help me figure out a problem. We have a very clear and intentional agreement about the form these conversations will take, and they're not coaching me.

It's acceptable—and very helpful—for you to disclose in real time what's happening for you because otherwise, the person will have some sense that there's something off, and they're going to make up a story about it. If I was feeling anxious and distracted, they might think, "Oh, you know, there's something different about Robert today. I can't even put my finger on it." But they may also think that I don't care. That I'm bored, that I'm just pretending to pay attention.

Coaching is a *form*.
Therapy is a form too. The boundaries are sometimes fuzzy. I ask myself whether or not I can be *helpful* and whether or not I have an *explicit agreement* with my client to go where I think we need to go. If I can't be helpful or we don't have that agreement, I'll do my best to encourage them to create an agreement with someone who can help them. I'll refer them to a therapist.

Boundaries are forms, and most boundaries are negotiable. Some are not (it's never appropriate, for example, for a coach to have sexual relations with a client). Boundaries are something we agree to. Some people negotiate the boundary: "Hey, I don't want to hear about your personal life other than, 'How you doing? Good? Good.' Then we're fine. Let's get down to work."

That's a boundary.

I don't have that boundary. I typically don't work with those clients very long because that doesn't interest me.

My clients can talk about anything they want. They can go as deep as they want to go. Our conversations can be personal, professional, tactical, strategic—or spiritual. We can talk about what they will say to their team in their meeting on Monday morning. Or we can plumb the mysteries as profoundly as they want to go, if that's what's calling them, right down to the existential ground of being, of essence.

CLIENTS AND FRIENDS

It is a bit tricky when you start seeing clients outside of a coaching container.

One of my clients asked me, "What if I decided I didn't want to do any more coaching; I just wanted to be your friend?"

"I already consider you a friend," I answered. "When I coach you, this is your time, and you're paying me because we have an agreement that we're going to exchange some value, and you're paying me for that exchange of value. We have a clear intention and container around that. If we started seeing each other outside of this container, that would be fine. It wouldn't change the fact that if we do coaching work together, we have a clear intention and agreement. If you told me, 'Robert, we've become such good friends, let's stop doing the coaching.' I would say, 'If you feel you got what you wanted out of coaching and want to stop, that's fine. We can be friends. But to be honest with you, I really love coaching. And so, I'm going to fill up a lot of my life with coaching, which means I have limited time for my friends. I'm happy that we're friends, but I won't be as available to you.'"

He decided to continue with coaching.

[COACHING FROM ESSENCE]

A big part of what I'm trying to teach people is to disentangle themselves from forms that don't serve them, learn how to navigate forms, and ultimately create forms that are more congruent with their essence.

Coaching is a form. We make an agreement. We're creating a thought form together. Part of creating that form is a negotiation. We agree, and as long as we have an explicit agreement, then we have a healthy form because then we can show up in that form positively and productively. When we're unconscious about the forms we create, that's when we create negative forms, dysfunctional forms, or contaminated forms that entangle us.

When you offer to coach a friend, you're creating a form. You want to create a very clear and intentional form.

I have a friend who always enjoyed engaging me in deep conversations bordering on coaching. I would say, "Hey, you know, I have some thoughts about that. Would you like to hear them?" I would ask for permission first.

Then one day, he said, "Listen, I think I'm interested in coaching. Could we do coaching?"

"Sure," I said. "But if you want to do coaching, two things. One, you have to pay me; there has to be a clear understanding that there's going to be an exchange of value, and then I'm just going to show up for you as a coach. And two, we need to create a coaching container. We're going to set up a time when we get together that's not about being friends and shooting the breeze. We're going to meet with a clear intention that I will coach you."

We did my coaching commitment of three months. After that, he felt he had enough to work on (he was doing a startup) and wanted to take a hiatus. I don't know how long it was—six months or a year later—and he said, "Hey, you know, I think I want to do some coaching again."

[CLIENTS AND FRIENDS]

In the meantime, we'd been friends and doing things together socially. But when we agreed to coach, we created a coaching container, and he paid me. He acknowledged that I was providing value for him, and we were very intentional about creating a space together, just for coaching.

COACH ABOVE YOUR LEVEL

Some coaches think you can only take a client as far as you've gone yourself.

That's not true.

Sometimes you have to take on a client that demands you go further than you've gone before.

One of the best ways to get better as a consultant and coach, and one of the secrets of practice building, is this: *Whenever a client asks you if you can do something, say yes.* Then figure out how to do it.

The only time you can say no is if you know you won't be able to figure it out (you're not trying to set yourself or the client up for failure) or when you know it won't meet The Essence Questions (you won't love it, it won't be of service congruent with your essence, or you won't like who you'll become).

Have I ever said no? Yes. Have I ever said yes and "failed"? Yes.

But you don't know what you're capable of until you try.

You're certainly capable of more than you think you are. I do things all the time that I don't know how to do—until I do them.

If you want to create B-prime for your clients and not just

[COACHING FROM ESSENCE]

recreate the success you already know how to create, you have to take the risk of doing something you're not entirely sure you can do.

BE A ONE ROOM SCHOOLHOUSE

As you trade up in your coaching practice, it's tempting to narrow the focus of who you work with. Maybe you *only* work with executives, or women, or people who show they are willing to do deep personal work. This can be a mistake.

Working with one kind of client can help you hone your skills in a particular area, but it can also create a closed network of people and ideas. It may reduce the chances of serendipity.

At the beginning of my practice, I accepted anyone who showed some motivation to do the work, especially if they offered to pay me. I soon clarified my ideal client by listing what about certain clients made me love them and what I didn't like about clients I didn't enjoy working with. Once that became clear, I tried to keep the door closed to those who were working on something that didn't interest me.

My practice now is a one-room schoolhouse. What matters most to me of all the criteria for my ideal client is that I enjoy working with the person and that they show up for the work. They're engaged, and they're benefiting from the work we do.

Within that broad criteria, I've coached CEOs, an architect, a nurse, over a hundred entrepreneurs, a real estate developer,

[COACHING FROM ESSENCE]

countless high-tech workers of various levels, and a handful of executives who were going through a transition. Some of them put everything on the table. The conversations were wide-ranging—personal and professional, tactical and strategic, sometimes vulnerable or spiritual. Others were strictly tactical. I was a thinking partner helping them solve problems.

You will enjoy working with some clients more than others, and you don't have to work with people you don't enjoy working with. But be careful not to focus your practice too narrowly. You can learn from everyone.

GIVE YOURSELF AWAY

I BELIEVE VERY strongly that it's important to do pro bono work, even if you're a very experienced coach. I believe this for several reasons.

First, you have to get good. And to get good, you have to practice.

Second, you have to start building a network, and the more people you talk to, the more people you work with, the more you optimize for serendipity. When people have powerful experiences, they tend to talk about them. That's how you create a practice that is one hundred percent referral.

Third, you have to *become* a coach. You have to change your identity. *A coach is someone who coaches.*

Finally, pro bono coaching is *big heart practice*. Pay the universe in advance, come from abundance, be generous with your being, and you will be surprised how quickly opportunities begin to show up for you.

When I first started my Coaching From Essence practice, I did mostly pro bono coaching. I would coach anyone and everyone. If I enjoyed the first session, I would offer them three or more sessions pro bono. I knew at the outset that most of

[COACHING FROM ESSENCE]

these people couldn't afford to pay me anything and would never become coaching clients. Some of them could have paid less than my full fee—and I could have pitched that—but when I started, I didn't think that way. I was trying to become a $10,000-a-month coach and had some other income, so I didn't need the money. I felt better knowing I could afford to work with someone pro bono, so if they could only afford a small fee, I didn't ask for it. If they offered me money, though, I always accepted whatever they offered.

Don't do pro bono coaching with the same person forever. You want to spread your love around.

If you want to create a solid coaching alliance, remember this: *you are always teaching people how to treat you.* Some people will not respect the work if they're not paying. Don't work with anyone who doesn't respect you, themselves, or the work.

When I'm working with someone pro bono, I tell them they need to show up powerfully. They need to take responsibility for themselves. If they say they will do something, they need to do it. They have to commit.

They have to show up. If they don't, stop working with them.

V

BE THE HOST

Every show I play, whether it's for an audience of 15,000 or 50, I look at it as a party, and I'm the host.
—Tyler Farr

BE THE HOST

You already know how to be a great coach. You also know how to solve any problem you have and how to create anything you want to create. You just don't know that you know.

When you're solving a problem or trying to create something, you do something and get a result. If it's not the result you want, you try something else and get a different result, and you keep repeating that process until you get what you want—or give up. It's trial and error. Tips and tricks. You don't change your goal, but you do change your strategy.

SINGLE-LOOP

[COACHING FROM ESSENCE]

It's called *single-loop learning*.
If the result isn't what you want, try something else.
And that's how most people think of creating—or coaching. Coaching is a set of competencies, best practices, good habits. Learn these five or seven or ten skills, and you'll be good to go.

If you try single-loop learning long enough and you're still not getting the results you want, you can back up and ask, "Wait a minute. How am I thinking about this problem or situation? What's my frame? What question am I trying to answer?"
That's *double-loop learning*.

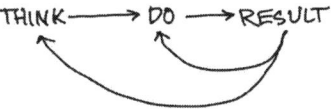

If you're still not getting the desired results, change the way you *think*.

If you change how you think about something, a different set of possibilities suddenly opens up. And that changes what you do, and that changes the results you get.

But sometimes, even changing the way you think doesn't go far enough.

If you're still not getting the results you want, you can back up even further and ask, "Who am I *being* in relation to this situation or problem or thing that I'm trying to create? What's

[BE THE HOST]

my intention here? What's my relationship to this thing? How

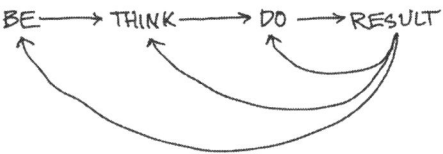

am I showing up?"

That's *triple-loop learning*.

If you've tried thinking differently and you're still not getting the desired results, try *being* different.

Changing who you're being changes how you think, the possibilities available to you, and what you do, which leads to different results.

There's no judgment about these; all three kinds of learning are helpful. But many of us mostly do single-loop learning. We get frustrated when we don't get the results we want. Sometimes we give up. If you're not getting the results you want, try changing the way you think about the problem or how you show up.

The solution to every problem you will ever face—and the key to creating everything you aspire to create—lies in one of these three loops: you will need to figure out what to do, how to think, and who to be.

Let me give you the simplest example I can think of.

Do you like networking events?

Most people don't like networking events, and yet, as a coach,

[COACHING FROM ESSENCE]

having a great network is one of the keys to your success. By some estimates, as much as fifty percent of your success depends on the quality of your network.

There are lots of tips and tricks about how to network. For example, you might try asking a different question than "What do you do for a living?" Maybe, "What are you excited about?" That might lead to a more exciting conversation. That's single-loop learning.

You might change the way you think about networking. Instead of trying to get as many business cards as you can, you might aim to have fewer, more meaningful conversations. That's double-loop learning, changing the way you think. You'll have a different experience depending on what you think you're doing when you network.

Or, you could . . . Just. Be. The. Host.

I don't even need to tell you how to do that. You already know how to be the host. If you showed up at a networking event and imagined that it was your event and you were the host, you'd think about it differently. You'd act very differently, and you'd have a very different experience.

Change the way you're being, and you'll change your results. That's triple-loop learning.

Coaching is being the host, creating a space where your client can show up as their best self and do their best work.

Leadership is also about being the host. And anyone in an organization can be the host.

Let me give you another example.

I designed and delivered the leadership track for entrepreneurs who attended several intensive programs on entrepreneurship, including the Global Startup Program, at Singularity University.

[BE THE HOST]

The meeting room was set up classroom style, with office chairs neatly arranged behind rows of long tables. I let them know we did things differently in the leadership course—that when I told them to begin, they were to rearrange the chairs in a horseshoe in the open space next to the tables. I would time them. The aim was to rearrange the chairs as quickly as possible without breaking anything or hurting anyone.

It usually only took two or three minutes. With everyone in their chairs, I'd stop the clock and tell them how they did. They were always pretty pleased with themselves, but I'd let them know that their time was *okay*. They'd have another opportunity at the next session.

Then I'd tell them about different ways to think about leadership, including triple-loop learning and being the host.

The next session, even before I took the front of the room, they'd ask if we were going to rearrange the chairs and if I was going to time them. I'd say, "Go!" They would rearrange the chairs, finally take their seats, the shuffling would cease, the room would hush, and someone would ask, "How did we do?"

"Great," I'd say. And pause. "But let me ask you something. If you were being the host, what would you do differently?"

It wouldn't take long for someone to say, "We'd rearrange the chairs before you got here."

The following week, the chairs were in a horseshoe when I arrived. More importantly, they began showing up for each other. Sometimes that looked like acts of kindness or generosity or going out of their way to help another entrepreneur solve a problem or make a connection. Sometimes it was just cleaning up after someone else because they wanted to take responsibility for creating a shared space where everyone could have the best experience. They captured these moments and posted photos or

[COACHING FROM ESSENCE]

anecdotes on their Slack channel, and they'd give each other kudos for being the host.

This sounds incredibly simple, but it can have a profound impact. In organizational literature, it's called *organizational citizenship behavior*, the things people do above and beyond their job responsibilities just because they want to be helpful. Unsurprisingly, it has a positive effect on performance.

Being the host is being accountable for creating a space where your client can show up as their best self and do their best work.

Together with your client, you create a container, a sacred circle—the biggest bottle you can conjure—so the client can experience their limitations and begin to stretch beyond them.

Many coaches think of this as *being with* the client. And you are. You sit, fully present, inside the container, inside the circle with them, with a powerful intention to hold whatever comes up.

Being the host is more than just *being with*; it's also *being for* the client. You are an ally and an advocate. You see the opera singer in them (remember Paul Potts?). You are holding not mere space but their highest potential.

You have to think, *How do I show up?* What do you need to hear and say and hold for the other person to bring their most powerful self to the coaching conversation they're having with you and for the conversation they're having with their life?

You already know how to be a great coach.

Be the host.

WHAT YOU KNOW IN YOUR BONES

You know something in your bones.
You knew it before you thought of becoming a coach.
You're not a *new* coach. There are no new coaches.
You have your life experiences. What you know in your bones is different from what I know in my bones—and every bit as valuable.
I tell you this because many people new to coaching will say, "Well, I'm a new coach, so I don't really know what I'm doing. Everyone else seems to have a bigger toolkit. They went to school. They're certified. They've *been* doing this. I don't have anything valuable to offer."
And that's *not true*.
Every model and tool in this book entered my life at the right time. Either it was something I learned and then adapted, or something I concocted out of desperation. What I know in my bones saved my life.
And you have that, too.
You have that already.
You have your human experience, your unique point of view, and your essence that will find its way. You know in your bones

what it is to have dreams. You know in your bones what it is to have a vision. You know in your bones the pain of having your essence stifled. You know in your bones the grief of losing something—your illusions, heartbreak.

You know what your life taught you.

Coaches love models. Clients love models. But models are not where the real work happens. The real work happens when two people create a connection based on trust, vulnerability, reliability, and integrity. What you know in your bones is more valuable to your clients than what you know in your head. To be firmly seated in your life experience, to ground your truth, to be solid, is a powerful place from which to coach.

That's valuable to your clients—not all of them, but some of them. Your *bone knowing* is precisely what someone needs to hear—and you will find each other.

I want to be very clear here: I'm not talking about bone *truth*, or *being right*, or the knowledge threshold (allowing what you know to prevent you from entering the unknown with enthusiasm). What we know in our bones may not be true, or it may only be true for us. It may not be wise; it may not even be helpful. But it is hard-won, it is human, and it is honest.

If you are to do deep work, you will have to bring your humanity—your bones—and not just your head, to your coaching. Head knowledge *and* bone knowledge is the difference between a coach who coaches only at the *doing* and *thinking* levels and a coach who also coaches at the *being* level.

Hold your tools and models lightly. Hold your bone knowing lightly, too. Your clients want someone who has conviction, who can speak with some authority about life, has a point-of-view (without being stubbornly opinionated), can assert themselves,

[WHAT YOU KNOW IN YOUR BONES]

and can challenge them in a way that allows them to show up more powerfully.

Bring your knowing to the conversation and help your client find what they know in *their* bones. You don't need any tools or models for that. You bring your curiosity and your humanity.

You've been preparing your entire life for every coaching conversation you will ever have.

You are *not* a new coach.

SIX COACHING QUESTIONS

There is no one right way to coach.

Every coaching conversation is a quest.

You're at a fork in the road every time the client stops speaking. There are always several options, and while some choices are better than others, there are no wrong choices. We don't know what will help the client until we try something, see how they respond, and try something else.

That doesn't mean we *only* have to wander and wonder.

What follows is a kind of map, but it's not a path. These six questions can help you find your way in any coaching conversation, but you'll rarely cover them in precisely this order, and sometimes you'll only ask a few of them. You might spend an entire session on one question. If you do ask all of them, you'll likely weave through them this way and that. If you drew the line you followed, it would look like an entwined thread.

That's okay.

[COACHING FROM ESSENCE]

Here are the Six Coaching Questions:

1. How can I help? *Agenda*
2. What's the current situation? *context*
3. What's the ideal scenario? *(success)*
4. Why don't you have it right now? *gap*
5. What *could* you do? *options*
6. What *will* you do? *commitment*

2q. Why is this a problem for you?
3q. what's your role in this.

Don't be attached to the wording of these questions; think of the intention.

1. *How can I help?* This question is about setting the agenda. What should we focus on? What's the most valuable thing we can talk about? When you first begin working with a client, in your enrollment conversation, you discuss all the particulars of your coaching alliance. That's a *contracting* conversation. At the beginning of each session, you agree on what you'll work on in that session. This question is a contracting conversation in miniature.

2. *What's the current situation?* This is about understanding context. It's also an invitation for the client to tell their story. This question is all about *curiosity*. You can listen for the Levels of Creation, which will help you understand how the client is contributing to the problem, getting in their own way, or where you might focus to have the most significant impact.

3. *What's the ideal scenario?* What would it look like if you found the perfect solution to this problem and the situation was exactly the way you wanted? What's the best outcome you can imagine? The most important thing at this stage is *clarity*, helping the client clarify their B.

4. *Why don't you have that right now?* This is a critical question. We have to look at what's in their way. Invite them to think of

[122]

[SIX COACHING QUESTIONS]

all the things that are missing or would have to be different in order to reach B. Here again, *clarity* is essential. Many clients will talk abstractly about what's in the way; help them be specific.

Whatever reasons they give for why they don't have—or can't have—the ideal scenario, if *they* aren't on the list, the list isn't complete. One of my favorite questions is, "How did you create, promote, or allow the problem to become a problem?" Or, "How do you keep yourself from having what you say you want?" There is always something they're doing or not doing that, if they stopped or started doing it, would help them create their ideal scenario. Make sure they're on the list.

5. *What* could *you do?* This is about getting *creative* and generating options. Ask the client what they've already tried. (You don't want to offer something and have them respond, "I tried that. It didn't work.") Ask them what they could do about the reasons they don't have their ideal scenario. What's *in* the way *is* the way. Then, you can offer your suggestions, expanding the possibilities.

6. *What* will *you do?* Of the options you've discussed, what actions will they take? What's the first domino? Invite them to *commit* to taking action, however small, but don't be attached to having the client take action—it isn't always about the *do loop*. Sometimes the step they need to take is to reflect on everything you've talked about.

You'll notice that these six questions lead the client through five distinct stages: *Contracting, Curiosity, Clarity, Creativity,* and *Commitment.* There is a certain logic to this order, but hold it lightly. Don't be afraid to wander and wonder. If you feel a conversation isn't productive, you can steer it back to these five stages and the Six Coaching Questions.

It's a good idea to *aim* to cover these six questions in a single session, ending on what they'll do, but don't force it. You may spend an entire session clarifying the ideal scenario or exploring the *real* reasons the client hasn't created that scenario.

Knowing these six questions will help you from getting lost in the weeds. If you do get lost, ask the Wayfinding question. . . .

THE WAYFINDING QUESTION

You will never be lost in a coaching conversation if you remember this Wayfinding question:

If you were to distill all of this down to a single question that you most wanted an answer to, what would the question be?

I have easily asked this question a hundred times. No one has ever responded, "I don't know." Somehow they always manage to crystallize their thoughts and ask a question that is either workable in the current conversation or something they can explore with renewed clarity after the session.

Keep the Wayfinding question in your back pocket. It is one of the most powerful coaching questions I know.

THE FIRST THREE SESSIONS

THE ANSWER THE client is looking for is almost always there right at the beginning. Often in the first session, the client is telling you what they *really* want to create—not in so many words, but in what's speaking—and it takes them time to work up the courage to act on their dream. Sometimes I'll invite the client in the first session to do what they need to do (start a new project, fire someone, etc.), but they're not ready to do it. They don't have faith in themselves, don't have the courage, or are too attached to self-interest, status-seeking, scarcity, and survival, and they won't let themselves take the risk.

The client knows what they need, but they don't know that they know—or they're not ready to let themselves know it.

A great coaching conversation is when both people get something they didn't know they needed and learn something they didn't know they knew. That's B-prime. Something unexpected happens that's better than they imagined.

In the first session, I allow a lot of time for them to explore their situation. It's important to let them tell their story and to listen with full presence and curiosity. After I understand the current situation, I ask them about their *ideal situation*. Almost always, the person will tell you a crippled version of their ideal scenario. In other words, they tell you what they want, but they also explain why they can't have it. I usually share the concept of A to B with them and then invite them to go on an adventure together.

It's essential to help them dream. What they dream is less important than the act of *dreaming*. Most people won't let themselves want what they truly want. They've been taught for so long to want something else, something someone else wants, or that they can't have what they want. The aim of the first session is to help them see that it is possible to create what they want, especially if it matches their essence.

As they tell me their story during that first session, I also reflect what I see and hear in their Levels of Creation. What are they telling me about their essence? Vision? Identity? Beliefs? Values? Capabilities? I usually do this without teaching the model (since I teach it later).

I then help them generate some options (I'm not afraid to help if they have option blindness) and commit to some actions. What's the first domino?

At the end of the first session, they should have clarity about their B, some openness to B-prime, and excitement about being on the journey with you. I've usually introduced the idea of the goose in the bottle, A to B, and how to knock over the Empire State Building.

In the second session, the goal is to get more clarity and put them to work. I often start by asking them a checking question: *What's different since we last spoke?* I ask this question because if people don't take inventory of what's changing, they often won't notice it. When they talk about what's changed, they already have a *feeling* of progress, even if the change is small.

They then usually give me an update and tell me a story of

[THE FIRST THREE SESSIONS]

what they're struggling with. This is when I introduce Levels of Creation if I haven't in the first session. I may also teach the Futurosity Continuum (especially if they're an executive, as they are more likely to relate to the language).

After the first two sessions, we should have some trust and momentum, a common language we can build on, and then our work is responding to the client and reminding them of their B.

Our job is to be patient. I tell my clients, "I can't tell you where you want to go. You go, and I'll follow you. I won't *push* you. But if you stop, I'll bump into you." And sometimes, I bump into them session after session. Eventually—because they've told their story enough times that the old story loses interest, or because the story takes on a new meaning, or because they have tipped over enough dominos that they are feeling inspired and a little bit cocky and maybe a little bit courageous, or maybe for some reason that neither one of us understands because we just got something we didn't know we needed—eventually, they start to move.

And then sometimes they move so fast it's hard to stop them. They may start *failing by succeeding*. They become so creative that they create many good things, but not the things they want. When we see that, our job is to be an honest mirror and show them where they are out of alignment.

THE ANSWER IS IN THE QUESTION

If you can't find the answer to a question, ask a different question.

That's double-loop learning.

Instead of persisting, when you can't seem to make any progress, change your thinking. Reframe the situation.

Sometimes people get attached to an unanswerable question and cling to it because it reinforces the way they're attempting to solve a problem that no longer exists. They are trying to prove to themselves that they aren't stuck, that they're doing the best they can.

Sometimes you have to help them find the Quest(ion) that can set them on a new path.

You're going to get an answer to the question you ask. If you can't find the answer you want, stop looking for it. Look for a better question.

A client once went on at length about his complicated and extremely challenging situation. I asked him the Wayfinding question: "If you were to distill all of what you've told me down to the question you most want an answer to, what would it be?"

He hesitated. "What do I do about this situation?"

[COACHING FROM ESSENCE]

Clients often want a single-loop solution to their problems. Unfortunately, in this case, the situation he referred to was entirely out of his control. I pointed that out.

"What's a question that's answerable?" I asked.

He smiled.

"How do I prepare my team for the worst?"

"That's better," I said. "At least you have some control over that. What's a better question?"

He paused, although not for very long. We'd played this game before.

"How can I think more strategically about these challenges and find whatever opportunities might be hiding here?"

I nodded.

DUCHAMP'S DOOR

Shortly after I completed the Hive program for leaders and entrepreneurs, Hive threw a party at their new digs in The Light House, a historic church transformed into luxury townhomes across the street from Dolores Park in San Francisco.

I had a long conversation with a brilliant young woman deciding what to do next in her life. She had numerous passions, several offers (from investment banking to politics to nonprofits), and was mulling over a few scholarship opportunities.

I can't remember many details of our conversation, but I can see it—vividly. I was sitting on the steps, and she was standing above me. People tumbled in and out of the Light House, Dolores hummed with passing cars, and the air was full of summer.

"Have you ever heard of Marcel Duchamp?" I asked.

"No," she said.

"He was an artist. In the corner of his apartment in Paris, there were two doorways and one door. To open one door was to close the other. If you keep all your doorways open, you're almost certain to bump into the door," I said. "You're trying to decide what door to open. What door are you going to close?"

Then she turned around.

"Oh, my god!" she said. "The doors."

Behind us were three grand doors. As she looked at them, she mused aloud about her options, picturing herself going through each door. I could hear, almost like music, the energy she felt for each. One was like a march, one an elegy, another a lullaby.

She didn't go through a door that day.

Instead, she went on a quest.

She did her research, spoke with people, visited campuses, and used her friends as sounding boards. And then, almost effortlessly, she made her decision. Or her decision made her.

Did she go through the right door?

We're not looking for the optimal path from A to B. I don't believe in optima, best solutions. That idea sometimes leads to paralysis by analysis and sometimes to regret.

We're not looking for the optimal path but a quest for something that is better than we can imagine. Holding that intention—that we are openly seeking something better than the inside of our bottle—gives gravity to B-prime and draws us to possibilities that otherwise would not be available to us.

Sometimes you come to a critical fork in a road that doesn't seem to lend itself to small experiments but requires a *leap of faith instead*. Yet, what feels like a leap of faith decision is often the result of many small, sometimes microscopic, experiments that have led you to the edge. There at that edge, even as much as you leap, sometimes it is a *fall of faith*; you simply surrender to what is calling you.

This is a conversation you are always having with your essence, with the life that wants to be lived through you.

Sometimes this leap—or fall—happens in a conversation

with a client. As you listen to the music of their story, you can reflect it back, and they'll resonate with the choice that is right for them.

Many of our choices are a B on the way to another B. We chose the school we attended because we hoped it would get us someplace we thought we wanted to go after school. We chose our particular job, hoping it would lead to our dream career.

But things don't always go the way we hope.

We're not always helping our clients make the best out of the hand they're dealt. Sometimes they unknowingly choose or inadvertently create B-sub. That's how they learn. It's what I call *succeeding by failing*—they have to make the wrong choices to learn how to make better choices.

If you're playing the game of self-interest, status-seeking, scarcity, and survival, the best thing that can happen is for you to "fail" at it. If you can learn from that experience, you are on the road to success (as I define it: living from essence, abundance, service, and trust).

Our role as coaches is to help people make better choices. Our role is also to help them learn more from "bad" choices.

There are tools and frameworks for choosing from multiple options, and the right tool depends on the person. Some people are naturally more path-like; some are more quest-like. Some decisions are more path-like (there may be one or only a few right choices among many options), and others are more quest-like (all the possibilities have merits that can't be foreseen until one goes on the journey. I think most of life's important decisions fall into this category).

I encourage clients to go on a quest, take small steps, explore, take any path, and begin learning what they don't know. To look—not for answers—but for the questions they didn't know to ask.

[COACHING FROM ESSENCE]

I often ask clients to put themselves in the future and describe it to me, like the woman who imagined walking through each door. Looking back from the future . . . *Have you created a life you love? Are you serving in a way that is congruent with your essence? Who have you become?*

Where we eventually find ourselves has a lot to do with serendipity. Think of the most important events in your life, perhaps a change in where you lived, went to school, where you worked, or how you met your beloved. Some of the most important events in our life are not choices but gifts.

What if you're coaching someone, and they're making one of those fork-in-the-road decisions that feel like a dice roll?

Answer: *Cradle the dice in both hands. Shake vigorously. Kiss your hands. Throw.*

If you're happy with your throw, go for it.

If not, *throw again.*

SPEAK YOUR CLIENT'S LANGUAGE

*O*NE CLIENT IS *an architect who wants to create her ideal firm.*
Another is a business development executive searching for his next career opportunity.
Another is a creative writer and designer mired in self-doubt about the upcoming marketing campaign for their new product launch.

My first intention is to understand the story my clients are weaving. I become inquisitive, drawing them out and demonstrating my understanding by summarizing what I'm hearing.

I listen carefully to the language they use to describe their situation. I listen for how they see themselves, what they believe, what they value. In the telling, they reveal their schemas, their way of organizing the world, how they make meaning, their Levels of Creation. I listen for where they place themselves in their story.

I ask the clients what they've thought of or tried. The answers aren't *the* answer (if they were, they wouldn't be asking for help), but I think I can build on them.

I have extensive experience helping clients move through

[COACHING FROM ESSENCE]

their problems, and I'm not a coach who shies away from giving clients advice when I think it's appropriate and would be helpful. I offer a few suggestions. I can tell they're not landing.

If you can't find the answer to a question, ask a different question. I say to the architect, "You're an architect. If your ideal firm were a building, what would it look like?"

Without hesitation, she pulls out a pen and a clipboard crammed with blank paper. Her hand dances over the page. She pauses, turns the clipboard, the pen hovers in the air, she tilts her head, then glides the pen around the page like an ice skater.

When she's finished, she shows me the diagram. I can't understand it, but she does. She describes it to me. It's clear as a blueprint in her mind.

I say to the business development executive, "How does that work? How do you go about finding partners for your company? Lay it out for me."

He pulls out his notebook. He draws columns down the pages, labels each one. Each column is a stage in the process. Down the columns, he lists the steps. He writes intensely. Finally, he looks up, turns the notebook around, and walks me through the process, pointing with his pen.

I'm not ready to go out and do business development after this brief tutorial, but I can tell it makes sense to him. It lights him up.

"Great," I say. "That's how you're going to find your next career opportunity."

With a bit of translation, he has an action plan.

The creative writer and designer is more challenging. I can tell she's feeling down. She's full of self-doubt, doesn't feel supported by her manager, and is struggling to find a voice that feels authentic. She's almost pleading with me when she says, "I'm stuck. I can't create. Nothing comes out."

[SPEAK YOUR CLIENT'S LANGUAGE]

I empathize.

After a moment of sad silence, I say, "Do you have a piece of paper and a pen?"

She's sheltered in place because of Covid-19, huddled in her bathroom for our Zoom call, the only place she can escape her kids and find the quiet to talk, but she scrounges around off-camera and returns with a sketch pad and a couple of markers. She looks expectantly at me.

"Can you draw what it feels like to be stuck?" I ask.

She picks up a marker, looks at the sketch pad for a long time with the marker suspended above the page, puts the marker down, picks up another one. Then, without hesitation, the marker dives down to the page, and she's drawing, pressing so hard I can hear it scratching the paper.

When she finishes, she holds up the drawing. It's a face with bars across the eyes and ears and mouth.

"It looks like see no evil, hear no evil, speak no evil," I say.

She sighs.

"You're not blocked," I tell her. "It's not true that you can't create. You have the evidence in your hands. You just had to pick up the right marker. Then you didn't even hesitate; you just did what you know how to do. Do that."

There's a faint smile.

It doesn't matter that the drawing is all about how she's blocked. She knows that *she* decides whether or not she can create.

We talk about how she can approach her manager. We talk about how she can find her authentic voice. I have a few suggestions, but mostly I don't have to say very much because she already knows. She knows herself and her manager better than I do.

I have a way of talking about my work that clients find valuable. I often share a few essential models with them in our first few sessions (A to B, Levels of Creation, Futurosity Continuum, and so on) to create a shared language about how we will work together to create what they are longing to create.

Sometimes, the easiest way to help your client solve a problem is to reframe it as a problem they already know how to solve.

Leave the tools in the toolbox.

Let them speak their native tongue—architecture, business development, or design. Ask the question in the language they know how to speak, and they will find their answer.

EVOCATION AND PROVOCATION

We need to do more than listen when we coach.

Good coaching is a combination of *evocation* and *provocation*.

Evocation is drawing the person out, evoking their story. We become intensely curious; we investigate. To evoke means to *call out*, to *summon*. We call them out, call up what's deep and hidden to the surface, and hold a space for them to befriend it. We conjure them up so they can see and imagine what they want to see and imagine.

But that's not enough.

We also have a responsibility to *provoke* them, stimulate them, awaken them. We sit outside their bottles (though we have bottles of our own). We can see how they limit themselves, hold themselves back, cling to obsolete forms.

Both *evoke* and *provoke* come from words that mean *to call*. When you evoke, you are calling your client on a journey. They can refuse the call. Provoke carries the connotation of challenge. When you provoke, they can still refuse the call, but you are calling them a bit more urgently.

When we provoke, we're not picking a fight. We're tapping—gently if we need to, more forcefully if we know our client is ready—on their bottle. We're helping them see how they're playing small, creating from the past, disconnected from their potential—or about to fall off a cliff.

I will tell my clients, "I have a provocation for you. Is that okay? Are you ready?" I've never had anyone say no.

"I'm not saying this is true," I'll say. "This isn't a diagnosis. This is a story I'm making up for you to play with. Maybe it will spark something for you."

A provocation is an invitation to come to the edge of their bottle, feel the glass, and look outside.

Tap lightly.

HOW (NOT) TO GIVE ADVICE

I'M A COACH who gives advice. Here's some:
It's never too early to start saving for retirement.
Be true to your teeth, and they'll never be false to you.
Never take love for granted.

There's a lot of debate about whether or not—and how—coaches should or shouldn't give advice.

Let me be clear about what I mean by advice. What is advice? Is it telling someone what to do?

No.

Here's one meaning of advice: *guidance or recommendations offered with regard to prudent future action.*

Hmm. That seems like it might be helpful to a client.

Let's go deeper.

The word *advice* comes from words that mean *to see*. The original meaning was a *way of looking at something*.

What are we doing when we give advice? We're giving our clients guidance from the point of view of the future. We're helping them *create* from the future.

More importantly, we're helping them see differently, to see something they wouldn't have seen on their own, no matter how much we asked questions or listened. We're offering a way of looking at something, a way that wouldn't be available to them without our input.

We may even be tapping on their bottle.

There is absolutely a time and place for advice, and it's our responsibility as coaches who aim to do deep, powerful work to give advice at the right time and place.

If you are jumping in with solutions without understanding the real issue, your advice won't be very helpful. That's why I encourage you to listen to your client's story and to be curious. Listen actively, paraphrasing thoughts and feelings so they can clarify their thinking and take their story deeper. If you have not listened, it is not the right time or place to give advice.

When is the right time?

The best time to give advice is when the client is clear about what they are creating and are ready to explore options. *What does B look like? What would an ideal solution look like? What could* they *do?* If you are giving advice before you clarify their answers, you may very well solve the wrong problem.

Ask them, "What have you already thought of or tried?" This is where I invite the client to figure things out. If they seem to have a good idea of how to handle the situation, I may encourage them and leave it at that.

Acknowledge their ability and resourcefulness to deal with the situation. Encourage them to explore possibilities with you, offering suggestions if you think they might help.

Pose the problem, praise the person, pursue possibilities.

If I offer my input, I'll say, "This isn't advice. I don't know you or the situation (or problem or other person or what you're trying to create) well enough to know if this is the right course of action. Here are some things to think about...."

Then I offer my suggestions and check in with them after each one.

You will never understand what your client is facing the way they understand it, but that doesn't mean you can't offer good suggestions. It does mean you have no way of knowing whether your suggestions are good. Your client knows if they're good. If they don't know, they can decide whether or not to try them. If they try your suggestions, they'll know.

Ask permission if you're uncertain or want to suggest something that might be edgy for your client. You can say, "Hey, I have a crazy idea here that might be helpful. Are you open to hearing something that might sound a little strange?"

Almost everyone will be willing to hear it, even if they say, "No, that doesn't resonate for me."

That's okay.

When I'm done giving advice, I remind them: "I can't tell you what to do. I don't know what's right for you. You have to try this on and see whether or not it resonates with you and decide what course of action is best for you."

There are things you know that others don't, and you can be courageous in sharing what you know. Not arrogant but courageous. You have an idea of right and wrong. You can see a cliff—strategic, moral, personal—that someone else may not be able to see.

As a coach, you have a responsibility to tell someone when you see something they don't see that may have dire consequences for them if they don't pay attention.

I'll give you a sad example of this. I had a client who was struggling in his business. He couldn't raise funds and went

[COACHING FROM ESSENCE]

deeper into personal debt to keep the company afloat. This is an incredible human being who has a lot of integrity and is very open and conscientious, but with some troubling blind spots.

I strongly encouraged him to look realistically at the situation and to decide what it would take for him to pull the plug. For months, I tried to help him work through his challenges, always offering things to think about and encouraging him to fold if things didn't get better. I encouraged him—strongly—to make a decision quickly so he could preserve resources and have the opportunity to try again.

In the end, he had to close the business and was hundreds of thousands of dollars in debt. When we spoke last, he had put his home on the market (at likely one of the worst times to do so).

Now I'm wondering: should I have voiced my opinion more strongly?

Note: I can't tell you what to do. I don't know what's right for you. You have to try this on and see whether or not it resonates with you and decide what course of action is best for you.

Nota Bene: The advice I gave at the top of this chapter was not an attempt at humor. If you ask me, I'll tell you. I know it in my bones. And the most profound bone knowledge I know is this: Never. Never, EVER. Never take love for granted.

VI

THE DARK ALLY

Hell is not punishment, it's training.
—Shunryu Suzuki

THE DARK ALLY

We've talked about failing by succeeding—getting so good at creating that you inadvertently create something you don't want.

You can also *succeed by failing*. Your life can fall so utterly apart that your shadow is sprawled before you, leaving you nowhere to hide.

This is often the work of the Dark Ally.

If you will not go to your demons, your demons will come to you.

You'll find that some clients come to you for coaching because they feel they're failing in their life. Not only are they not creating what they thought they wanted, but they've lost the thread—they have no idea what they want. This may be true on a personal level or a professional level. Many entrepreneurs face this dilemma on the way to bringing their creations to market. They become haunted by fear, uncertainty, confusion, exhaustion, and doubt. This is more common than you might think. It's almost universal (though, of course, it can vary by degree).

If your client has been playing the game of self-interest, status-seeking, scarcity, and survival, failing is the first step toward success. Even if they are trying to create from essence, abundance, service, and trust, if they are creating something that isn't congruent with who they are, failure is the path to creating a life they love.

Remember: *there is no failure, only lessons*. If we do not learn the lessons we need to learn the easy way, we will learn them the hard way.

The hard way is the way of the Dark Ally.

You will fail. Your clients will fail. Failure helps us learn what we need to learn to get right with ourselves, course-correct, find our way back, and find the right quest. *That* will put us on the path to success.

I've shared about my dark passage, how my life fell apart, and I came nose to nose with my shadow, my half-heartedness. I now know that this passage was absolutely necessary for me to get right with myself again. I don't know of any other way this could have happened. Without that failure, I would have failed by succeeding—I would have created a successful but half-hearted life.

If it sounds like we play a part in our dark passage—that we, in some sense, bring the darkness on our own heads—that is often (but not always) true.

There is a part of us that knows when we have veered so far from our center that we need a shock to wake us from sleep. I think of this part as our *longings*. If we begin to lose our way, they call to us gently. If we become lost, they may rattle us awake.

It's also true that some calls to adventure cannot be refused. The dark passage is not merely our confused, fragmented self muddying about, but the deep dark we have always feared was hiding under the bed.

It may seem spurious or naive to think that darkness

[THE DARK ALLY]

sometimes comes as an ally, but it assuredly does. Whether we have created the darkness ourselves, by some unknowable part trying unskillfully to bring us into the light, or whether the darkness visits us from the unknowable, existential ground of being—the darkness always has the potential to be a friend.

There is no easy answer to the darkness, and sometimes we need to refer a client to someone else for professional help.

It's not our place as coaches to protect people from their dark passage or to come between them and their Dark Ally. But we can stand with them in the shadow as a flicker of light.

TURN TOWARD EVERYTHING

Let me tell you a story about demons.

Milarepa was a Buddhist teacher. He spent a lot of time meditating in a cave. One day he left to gather firewood, and when he returned, he found the cave full of demons.

Nobody likes to come home to demons, so he tried chasing them away. What do you think happened? The more he chased them, the more they made themselves at home.

Being a teacher, he thought he would teach them the Dharma, the spiritual teachings of Buddhism. What happened? They just sat and stared at him.

Since single-loop learning wasn't working, he decided to look at the situation differently. So he sat down and said, "It looks like we're going to be here together. I open myself to whatever you have to teach me."

All but one of them vanished.

That one demon wouldn't leave.

How does Milarepa get rid of the last demon?

The demon—the *problem*—is not the problem. There will always be problems in your life.

[COACHING FROM ESSENCE]

The *response* to the problem is the problem.
And how you respond depends on what you think you're responding to.

Here's what life looks like most of the time:

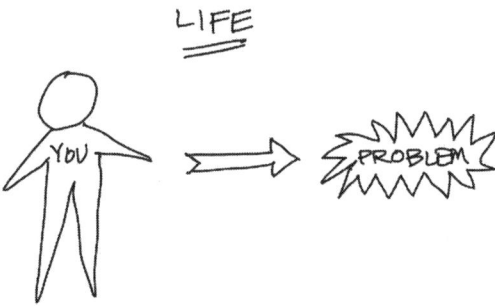

We're always dealing with one problem or another, sometimes very small problems. And most of the time, these problems are manageable. We can apply single-loop learning to them and do just fine. Here we are, and the problem is over there. It doesn't really bother us; it's just something that needs to be attended to.

Sometimes, we take on a problem and can't let go. We ruminate. We worry. Instead of the problem being outside of us,

[154]

something we can pick up or put down, we've taken it on, and it goes with us everywhere.

We live in an environment that's full of problems. Some people refer to this condition with the acronym VUCA, which stands for volatility, uncertainty, complexity, and ambiguity. It's a military term that became popular in leadership circles in the 1990s. Even today, you'll hear many references to the VUCA world we live in. But this idea is already almost thirty years old. It doesn't capture how many people feel today.

I think a better description of what we're dealing with is ... FUC*ED: fear, uncertainty, confusion, exhaustion, and doubt (I don't know what the K stands for).

When you're FUC*ED, the problem is no longer outside of you. The problem is no longer inside of you. When you're FUC*ED, *you're inside the problem*. The problem feels bigger than you; it's overwhelming.

Fear, uncertainty, confusion, exhaustion, and doubt are the demons that every one of us, sooner or later, must wrestle with.

FEAR

Fear is panic or anxiety.

What are you afraid of? *Write it down.*

What's the antidote to fear?

<u>It's courage</u>. Courage comes from a word that means *heart*. <u>The antidote to fear is heart</u>. When you love what you're doing enough, you won't be afraid. If you're hesitant, remind yourself how much you love what you're creating.

Some people become afraid, even when things are going well. They feel they don't deserve to be successful.

<u>*Do you deserve to be successful?*</u> Why do you deserve to be successful? (Pause for a moment and feel your answer to this question.) If you don't feel you deserve to be successful, there's a simple cure.

Deserve means *serve*. The word *deserve* literally means *to serve well*.

If you don't feel you deserve your success, serve more. <u>Find a way to create more value.</u>

Most big problems are the result of avoiding small problems. Are there small problems you've been avoiding that might turn into bigger ones? How can you keep small problems from becoming bigger problems in the first place?

Face your fears by doing a *premortem*.

A postmortem looks at everything that went wrong after the fact and tries to figure out how to do better next time. A premortem looks at all the things that could go wrong and figures out what to do about them *before* they happen.

Even if you're already overwhelmed with problems you're struggling to solve, take a look ahead and be proactive.

<u>*Find your allies.*</u> One of the best ways to deal with fear is to talk to someone you trust—a friend, mentor, or another coach.

It's easy to isolate yourself when you're feeling overwhelmed, but for most of us, that's the worst thing to do. Don't be afraid to ask for help. Encourage your clients to do the same. Your clients are fortunate to have you, but they also need the support of other important people in their lives.

UNCERTAINTY

Uncertainty is unpredictability, changeability, inconstancy.

If you're on a path and don't know where you're going, it's frightening. But if you're on a quest, you're not expected to know where you're going.

Separate what you know from what you don't know. Even when you're in a situation that's full of uncertainty, there are always things that you know, that you can rely on.

Make a list of what you know about the situation you're in. What are the facts? What can you rely on?

What don't you know? It's awful when you don't know what you don't know. But when you know what you don't know, you can turn what you don't know into a quest.

What's your Quest(ion)? What are you uncertain about that you could become certain about if you knew what you needed to know? Some things may remain unknown, but you can usually find out more by asking good questions.

CONFUSION

Confusion is disorder, chaos, jumble, mess.
  Confusion comes from words that mean *mingle together*.
  How do you deal with confusion? *Sort it out.*

[COACHING FROM ESSENCE]

Write down everything you're worried about. Get it outside of yourself. One way to do this is to write everything down on Post-it notes, one item per Post-it. You can sort them and look for patterns or categories. You can prioritize them. Maybe you (or your client) can delegate some of them.

Focus on your ideal scenario. Even when it seems more impossible than ever. When considering options, clarify what you want, what success looks like. What does a good decision look like? What does a bad decision look like? What do you need to know before you can make a decision?

What if it isn't a problem? Could what you think is a problem be the solution to a *different* problem?

Consider the Post-it Note. It wasn't what its inventor was looking for, so it could've been considered a failure, but it was a massive success in solving a different problem the inventor hadn't even considered.

Is there a solution to another problem that makes the current problem a nonissue?

Sometimes you're confused because you're stuck in a single loop, trying different things without understanding the problem. Try thinking about the situation differently or asking yourself if it's a problem with *being*, your intention, or how you're showing up.

EXHAUSTION

Exhaustion is fatigue, feeling used up.

Exhaustion is a common problem. The solution isn't easy, but it is simple.

You can manage your energy by taking better care of yourself. Here's a simple mnemonic: right STUFF.

Get enough *sleep*, control your *thoughts* (a meditation practice is invaluable), engage in the right *undertakings* (i.e., activities, like exercise), eat healthy *foods*, and find time for *friends* and *family*.

Whenever I'm talking with a client who is overwhelmed and exhausted (and sometimes they're feeling great about everything they're doing), I remind them of the importance of self-care. If you're crunched for time, find opportunities for micro self-care; take a nap, meditate for five minutes, eat a piece of fruit, call a friend. Every little bit helps.

DOUBT

Doubt is indecision, hesitation, vacillation, mistrust.

It's easy to get stuck here.

What are your voices of doubt? (Remember the Love threshold?)

You have to face your doubts. Write them down.

Don't believe your thoughts. Don't believe everything you think. If your thoughts are not helping you, challenge them. When you have doubts, ask yourself, "Is this true?" If you're not sure, is there a way to test what you're thinking?

If your thoughts aren't helpful, think someone else's thoughts for a while. Read a book. When you read a book, you're thinking someone else's thoughts, and it's one of the best ways to get yourself out of an unproductive thought loop.

I highly encourage you to have a daily meditation practice, even if you only have five minutes. Notice your thoughts.

If you pay attention, you'll notice that most of your thoughts fall into one of three categories: memories, fantasies, or stories.

Memories. Usually, regret over something you've done in the past or nostalgia—longing for better times.

Fantasies. Imagining how great it will be when everything works out, or imagining how you'll solve a problem, or imagining that you'll say (or said) the perfect thing to someone.

Stories. Making up reasons things are the way they are, why someone did whatever they did, why you're constantly fucking up, etc.

None of these thought patterns are particularly helpful—unless you're looking to the past for lessons that might be applicable now, you're imagining possible scenarios in order to come up with more creative options, or you're making up stories to test different theories. When I was stuck in a dark place and first noticed these patterns, I began repeating this mantra: *no memories, no fantasies, no stories.*

Free yourself from the outcome. One of the reasons we get stuck in indecision and hesitation is that we're too attached to outcomes. We fear the worst.

Here are two experiments that prove the point:

In the first, researchers asked people to jump out of airplanes—to skydive, not once, but three times—and measured their cortisol levels before and after each jump. After the first jump, the stress levels were cut by about a quarter. After the third jump, *the stress levels were only about half of the first jump.*

In another experiment, researchers measured the stress levels of ballroom dancers. They were measured before and after each competition—tango, waltz, foxtrot. And guess what happened? *Their stress levels remained unchanged.* It didn't matter how experienced they were. Dancers who had competed for more than ten years were just as stressed as those with only a couple of years of experience.

Jump out of an airplane where you can die, and your stress

level goes down the more you do it. Compete in a ballroom dancing competition, where I'm pretty sure death is a long shot, and it's as stressful as something that could kill you.

Why?

If you're skydiving, as dangerous as it is, you have some feeling of control. You have all your safety rituals and can focus on what you need for survival. Jumping out of an airplane is an act of faith, of trust.

But when you're ballroom dancing, you're going to be judged. You can lose. No one will judge you if your parachute doesn't open up. They may think you're a loser, but it won't matter. If you screw up on the dance floor, it will. Your ego isn't involved when you jump out of a plane, but it's on the line when you're on the competitive dance floor. Competition is the ultimate stage for self-interest, status-seeking, scarcity, and survival.

So. Are you skydiving or ballroom dancing? Are you all in and focusing on what you need to do, or are you looking over your shoulder to see what other people think of you?

Do the work and let go of the outcome and what other people think.

The cure for depression is anxiety.

You have to do the thing you're afraid to do. You have to take action.

You don't have to do everything at once. You don't have to face all of your demons simultaneously. You don't have to knock over the tenth domino. Just knock over that first domino. Face the closest demon. Take the biggest, smallest action you can take. Big enough to be meaningful, small enough that success is assured.

One small demon, er, domino. Then another. Then another.

[COACHING FROM ESSENCE]

Remember Milarepa?

He tried to chase his demons away, but they became more entrenched.

He tried to teach them, and they just sat and stared.

He opened himself up to what they could teach *him*, and all but one disappeared.

But how did he get rid of the last demon?

He said, "Eat me if you wish," and put his head in the demon's mouth.

At that moment, the biggest demon bowed and dissolved into space.

What do you make of that?

Whenever you let yourself fully feel your feelings, *they always change into something else*. What we resist persists.

When you face your demons head-on, when you face the worst thing that can happen to you, you're free. Don't turn away.

Turn toward everything.

OUR WORK AS HUMAN BEINGS

B<small>ACK IN THE</small> mid-80s, I led personal growth workshops and retreats. I was in my mid-twenties. My father had died a few years before, and while I didn't know it at the time, I was doing everything I could to make sense of my loss, my unfinished business, and to find my way.

I had finished a master's degree in counseling from the University of Colorado in Colorado Springs, and I traveled monthly from Colorado to Indiana (where my brother lived and where I slowly built a following that met for workshops) to Detroit (where I stayed with my mother and created a community that met for a weekend retreat every month).

One of the posters I used to promote my workshops was roughly painted with a coarse, fat brush. It read: OUR WORK AS HUMAN BEINGS IS TO TRANSFORM OUR PAIN INTO SOMETHING BEAUTIFUL.

The fine print read: This is #1 in the *These Words Mean Everything They Cannot Say* poster series by Robert Ellis. There was also pricing, just in case you wanted to buy a copy, and my address. I sold ten copies, in total, to a gym (which seemed fitting but wasn't quite what I had in mind when I created it).

My work then was my way of transforming my pain into something beautiful. Coaching From Essence is also my way of transforming my pain into something beautiful. You will find, as I have, that people who are doing meaningful work are often working to make meaning out of a painful experience. What we learn from a dark passage becomes bone knowledge. If you listen for it, you'll hear this transformation in many stories of entrepreneurs, teachers, and activists.

On the reverse side of my poster was a kind of manifesto. Here's what it said:

As a teacher, and as a human being, I am concerned with learning and teaching what I learn about how we can begin to live the life that is trying to live itself through us. What does that mean? It means that I believe we are alive for a purpose, and that purpose is to remember that we are love. I believe that all of us love each other, whether we are aware of that or not. And that all of us are infinitely lovable, whether we know it or not. And that no matter what it is we think we are doing, all we are ever really doing is working on ourselves. And that work is to learn how to remember and experience and express and embody that love.

How do we begin?

We begin by becoming a conscious and willing instrument of life. We become willing to feel the feelings that want to make themselves felt through us, willing to be aware of the insights that want to be known in us, willing to touch what wants to be touched by us, and willing to create what wants to be created through us.

Our work is simple.

Our work is to inhabit our bodies and to be as fully aware as we can be. Our work is to learn everything we can about how we can open ourselves fully to the experience and creative expression of what is true for us, the full range of our sensations, feelings, thoughts, and

[OUR WORK AS HUMAN BEINGS]

inspirations. That doesn't mean that we will always act on all of these experiences. It is enough to feel our anger and fear, for example, we don't need to hurt anyone or run away from life. When we allow ourselves to be fully aware of all that we are feeling and that others are feeling, we can begin to be conscious cocreators in the unfolding mystery of life.

Our work is not easy.

Whatever we lie to ourselves about, whatever we hide behind, whatever we use to bolster ourselves, is in the way. We have to give up having all of the answers, trying to control others, manipulating everything to go a certain way. We have to begin afresh, stop pretending that we know others or even ourselves. To be reborn, we have to rediscover our innocence. There is nothing to be ashamed of. We don't have to be afraid of each other. We don't have to be afraid of ourselves.

There are no experts in this work. None of us know how to do it. All of us are doing the best we can. Doing it wrong is, in itself, the only penalty. Doing it right is, in itself, the only reward. And it doesn't matter how often we forget or how often we remember. Each moment we begin anew.

A GOOD DAY

I have stage IV prostate cancer.

When I got my diagnosis on November 14, 2017, everything in my life instantly changed.

And everything remained the same.

I was still me. I still had plans for the future. I didn't know how long I had to live before my diagnosis, and I didn't know after.

Here's one thing that changed: *instead of waiting for something to happen for me to be happy, I decided I had to figure out how to be happy every day.*

I used to think, *I'll be happy when I make a million dollars. I'll be happy when I have the opportunity to present in front of large audiences. I'll be happy when I write a book. I'll be happy when I find the perfect house.*

As incredible as all of those things are, in the happiest life, they don't happen every day. I wanted to know what would make me happy *every* day.

I made a list. The list became a mantra.

Here's my mantra: *love, laugh, learn, earn, move, dance, meditate, create.*

[COACHING FROM ESSENCE]

If I do even one or two of these things every day, it's a good day.

Michèle taught me how to start every day by checking off the first two. When I wake up in the morning, before we get out of bed (or if we've gotten out of bed at different times, we go back to bed), I make eye contact with my beloved. Within a few seconds, we're usually laughing.

I'm not as good at moving or dancing or meditating every day, but I don't think I've had a bad day since the day I got the news.

I don't always start by talking with my clients about what makes a good day for them, but it often comes up in conversations when they're stressed. While we're on the journey to B, we don't want to put our happiness out somewhere in the future.

What would it take for today—and every day—to be a good day? What's your mantra for a good day?

I want every day of your life to be a good day for you.

A MAJOR CHORD

"*A* MAJOR CHORD *is when everything in your life works out perfectly, when you have everything you could ever possibly want. Everything. You have the woman you want, you have the music you want, and you have enough money to live comfortably. That's a major chord.*"

The quote above is Robert De Niro speaking to Liza Minnelli in Martin Scorsese's movie *New York, New York*.

I saw this movie in the theater when it was first released in 1977. For some reason, this scrap of dialogue has stuck in my head for over forty years.

When I was going through my dark passage, as my life was falling apart and I was trying to piece it back together, I remembered the idea of a major chord and asked myself, *What would it look like for my life to work out perfectly?*

This is what I came up with:

–Lover/partner
–Friends and family
–Work and purpose

—Health

—Home

At the time (the summer of 2015), I was heartbroken and alone, had few close friends, was completely unsatisfied with my work, struggled with heart problems, and was about to lose my apartment.

I'm still working on my major chord, but since the summer of 2015, I met and married my beloved, I have a wider circle of amazing friends (and I include some of my clients in that circle), I love my work, I'm more creative and productive than I've ever been, I make more money than I've ever made, and I live in my dream home in paradise. I'm still working on the health thing, but even with Stage IV prostate cancer, I can honestly say I've never been happier.

We have to be careful when we help our clients clarify their B. Their B doesn't exist in isolation.

If our client has a big B for their business, it's reasonable to ask them what they're doing to take care of themself and their beloved while working one hundred hours a week.

Asking them what their major chord would be, what would make for balance between the things that are most important to them, can be a provocative question.

What would be a major chord for you?

What would it take for your life to work out perfectly?

FAILING BY SUCCEEDING

ONE REASON WE do personal as much as professional work with our clients is that without the personal side, they may create something they don't want. They may be achieving their ambitions and creating wealth and fame. But they may be only striking one note of their major chord very loudly (or not have a major chord at all). They hit that single note—achievement, money, fame—over and over again.

If you or your clients are playing the game of self-interest, status-seeking, scarcity, and survival, you may find that winning at that game is actually losing. It won't make you happy. It's what I call *failing by succeeding*. As the saying goes, you work hard to climb the ladder only to discover it's leaning against the wrong wall.

This can happen even if you pursue essence, abundance, service, and trust. At the beginning of 2020, just before the coronavirus struck, I had more clients than ever. I was well on my way to making over half a million dollars, which would have been my best year. I was happy about the money, but I wasn't happy about all the work. I realized that I had been saying yes to everything that came my way, whether or not I felt it was a good fit. As successful as I was, I was beginning to love what I was creating less than I wanted. I wanted to be of more service.

All of this may sound like an excellent problem to have. But I had been so gratified by my life the previous couple of years that I was beginning to feel out of balance. I was starting to feel trapped. I was succeeding financially but becoming less happy, feeling I had no time or energy for other important things. I wasn't creating the life I wanted. I was failing by succeeding.

We all know what happened next. Like many when the world shut down from COVID-19, I lost half of my business overnight—speaking engagements, leadership training, and coaching contracts. I thought I would have to cancel the Coaching From Essence programs.

I'm making less money now but enjoying my work more. I'm creating work that is more congruent with my essence.

Don't let your clients succeed at something that won't create a life they love, that won't allow them to use their essence to serve, that won't lead them to become the kind of person they want to be. When you see that they are failing by succeeding, lead them into a deeper conversation about the life that wants to live through them.

GIVE EVERYTHING TO EVERYTHING

Give everything to everything.

If you are just beginning and you're certain you are an impostor, give everything to everything.

You may be hesitant, lacking confidence. You may be afraid of saying the wrong thing (you may say the wrong thing). You may be certain you're not good enough. You may be bored. You may know halfway through the session that you don't want to work with this client and never want to see them again. You may feel out of your depth, feel yourself shrinking, stumbling over your words. You may forget everything you've learned, your mind clear as a window.

Give everything to everything.

Give your heart, give your bones, give your being.

I'm not talking about perfection. If I were talking about perfection, there would be no Coaching From Essence.

This journey is not a path to perfection; it's a quest for wholeness.

I'm talking about exposing all of yourself to the thing you do, to the person you're with, to the moment unfolding.

Sometimes, people will come to you because they're looking

for a way out—of a relationship, or a job, or their partnership, or their investors, or their leadership position. They may have any number of reasons for wanting to escape, most of them no doubt true. They may be uncertain, hesitant, tentative, full of fear—and longing. They may fall back on survival instincts, may want to hoard their being, shelter their heart in place, pull back, withhold, ration their presence, do as little as possible until they maneuver their way out.

This is a mistake.

Whether you are just beginning something or biding your time until something comes to its inevitable end—even if you are fully FUC*ED and overflowing with fear, uncertainty, confusion, exhaustion, and doubt—give everything.

Give everything to everything.

The best way to know if a relationship, a job, a cofounder, your investors, or your position as a leader—or as a coach with a client—is right for you is to give everything to everything. Then see what meets you, and you'll know. The situation will become clear—it's time to go—or it will transform into something different and better than you imagined.

I always tell a client who is half-hearted, lacking in confidence, or groping for a way out of a bad situation (and I've had many clients come to me, lost in the labyrinth, looking for an ally), "Give everything to everything. Don't hold back. Do your best and see what meets you. If nothing else, show *yourself* what you're worth. Steel your being so you can hold your presence in any situation. Turn toward everything—until it's time to turn away. *If you are half-hearted anywhere, you are half-hearted.*"

It's not about perfection, persistence, or proving yourself. It's about being your best self always, to the best of your ability. If

[GIVE EVERYTHING TO EVERYTHING]

you feel what you're doing is futile, if you feel your thoughts are unappreciated, focus on *being*.

Who are you becoming if you let yourself show up any way other than as your best self?

This is not about doing what you don't want to do. It's not about being a martyr. Not everything is right for you.

It's not about commitment. It's not about stubbornly pressing on. Things come to an end. You will outgrow your bottle and long for a bigger bottle. When you know that, it's time to go.

Until you go, give everything to everything.

When you go, give everything to everything.

THE ADVANCED PRACTICE

Gratitude is a powerful practice. The benefits are well-researched. Gratitude will help you feel better, savor positive experiences, improve your health, be more resilient, and create strong connections.

When I was stumbling through my dark passage, I kept coming across the recommendation to keep a gratitude journal. Reluctantly, I did keep a journal. Sometimes, my gratitude blindness was so thorough I had nothing to write. On other days it wasn't much better.

Here's an excerpt from my entry on December 21, 2014:

> *The sun came out today (went for a short walk around the neighborhood, then another at the Berkeley Marina)*
> *Whole Foods (expensive, but they're very friendly in there)*
> *Clouds (I love the clouds after we've been having rain)*
> *Pistachio nuts (bought some in the shell, yum and fun)*
> *It's solstice (now the days get longer and lighter, my dark passage will be ending soon . . . please God)*

Keeping a gratitude journal does help. I sometimes

recommend the practice to my clients. But I consider practicing this kind of gratitude the *beginner's practice*. It's easy, if you're paying attention, to be grateful for the good things that happen in your life. The advanced practice of gratitude is to be grateful for *everything* that happens in your life.

Though most people think of gratitude as *thankfulness*, it has a deeper meaning. Gratitude is derived from the Latin word *gratia*, meaning *grace, graciousness, or gratefulness*.

Gratitude is also related to the word *gratis*, meaning *free from cost*. When I offer to do my initial session with a prospective client, I let them know that I'll do the session *gratis*—free from cost—but what I'm really thinking is that I'll do the session *gratus*, meaning *grateful*—with gratitude.

It is a privilege to coach someone, a privilege we should approach with gratitude. If you aren't feeling grateful for the opportunity to coach someone, they're not the right client for you (no blame on you or them), and they will be grateful if you let them find the right coach for them.

I used to think I should work with anyone who showed up and be grateful for the opportunity. Now I realize I sometimes took that idea too far. I'm grateful for everything that shows up in my life over which I have no control (advanced gratitude), considering any adversity a Dark Ally. I am also grateful for my ability to choose, to discern for myself what feels right for me and wrong for me, without judgment (without labeling it good or bad).

Be grateful for what shows up for you. Be grateful for your choices. Most importantly, express your gratitude. Tell people. Call them. Write to them. When you begin to express your gratitude, it slowly transforms into something else....

Generosity.
What is generosity?

[THE ADVANCED PRACTICE]

One meaning of generosity is *noble birth*. And what does it mean to be noble? *Having or showing qualities that other people admire.* It also means *being abundant, more than adequate.* There's also a meaning, from the Classical Latin *noscere*, meaning *to know or to meet*.

Isn't that interesting?

We might think, then, that being generous is a way of putting others first, of coming from abundance, and a way to know or to meet people where they are.

Even on a cloudy day, when the world feels dark, we can be grateful for clouds and the sun and Whole Foods and pistachios and the realization that today is the solstice and the days will be getting longer and lighter.

But generosity is something else. Generosity is something much more profound.

Generosity is not about money—that's the beginner practice of generosity. It's not about doing pro bono work (anyone with time on their hands can offer to do a free session).

It is not so easy to be truly generous. It is not so easy, when we are generous, *to give everything to everything*, to be generous with our heart, our bones, and our being. It is not so easy to hold the other in admiration, create a space large enough for their abundant being, give them our attention so we may know and meet them, and open ourselves to being known and met.

That's what makes generosity the advanced practice.

And that makes for powerful coaching.

VII

THE ULTIMATE PRACTICE

*[To] make the patient feel better
before taking the medicine is
the most direct method.*
—Xu Shu-wei

THE MOMENT INSIDE THE MOMENT

RUSSELL HOBAN WAS my uncle. He wrote a collection of essays entitled, *The Moment Under the Moment*:

> *[The] moment under the moment, can't be put into words; the most that a writer can do . . . is to write in such a way that the reader finds himself in a place where the unwordable happens off the page. There is something wonderful and unexpected waiting for us when we let go of our expectations and listen carefully to what's present in the moment.*

In *The Wise Heart*, Jack Kornfield quotes psychologist Len Bergantino, describing a particular therapy session he had with a frustrated patient:

> *The feeling I had on this particular day was I just didn't want to say one more word to him about anything. So, to his surprise, I took out my mandolin and in the most loving mellow beautiful way I could, I played "Come Back to Sorrento." He broke down in tears and cried for the last forty minutes of the session, saying only, "Bergantino, you sure earned your money today!"*

[COACHING FROM ESSENCE]

I've never played the mandolin for anyone (I've never played the mandolin), but I've walked the streets of San Francisco for hours with a client and lounged on a park bench, watching kids play and dogs lifting their legs and cars idling by, while my client let his story go and realized a hidden truth that opened a way forward. I've sat on a bench with a client in the lobby of a luxury hotel in Europe and held silence inside our cocoon as people thrummed around us, leaned in, and spoke in whispers while tears streamed down her face as she recognized, underneath her story, how she was the solution to a problem that no longer existed.

Moments like these are not always accompanied by watery eyes or profound realizations but by the sudden awareness of the fullness of the moment in which we are held.

A veil parts, a weight is lifted, the smoke clears.

We recognize that the moment has a gift for us (as all moments do), and—somehow—we become attuned to the gift, receptive to it. Something completely unexpected and completely necessary happens before we can get in our way, keeping the gift at bay or letting it pass unnoticed.

What I'm talking about is rare, inexpressible, "unwordable." It's not the moment under the moment I'm after when I coach, but the moment *inside* the moment, not something that happens "off the page" or elsewhere, but the thing that most wants to happen *now*.

I sometimes think about everything that had to have happened to be in conversation with a client, how miraculous to share any precious moment with another human being, and how privileged we are to be together. History and longing and accident and serendipity have led us to each other, and now we sit as witnesses to our stories, and the moment, and the moment

[THE MOMENT INSIDE THE MOMENT]

inside the moment—the recognition that there is something special about this time we share.

If you have witnessed a birth or a death, lost your virginity, had a spiritual awakening—or undergone any rite of passage—you have an inkling of what I mean. Any moment can be as full, as mysterious, or as transformational.

Here you are, almost at the end of this journey within a journey to becoming the coach you want to be, and I'm telling you this: *you have to know when to let go—of your tools, your identity, your doing, and your thinking, all desire, all attachment to outcome—if you are to find the potential for every moment to be B-prime, to be better than you can imagine.*

The moment inside the moment is always available and always profound, but that doesn't mean it is always the aim of our coaching. Sometimes we are unraveling stories or problem-solving. Sometimes, as the Buddhist saying goes, we chop wood and carry water.

To find the moment inside the moment requires attention—mindfulness—a fullness of presence, a lack of effort, an acceptance, a waiting, a holding, a letting go. Become the kind of person who has no resistance to essence, and moments like these will become more possible. It will happen.

You'll know when it does.

THE ULTIMATE PRACTICE

Gratitude is the beginner's practice. It opens you up; it's a first step away from self-interest, status-seeking, scarcity, and survival. Feeling gratitude can shift your perspective and give you a glimpse of what life looks like outside your bottle.

If you take an inventory, you may discover you have more than you need. You begin to feel abundant, overflowing. If you continue to open yourself, you *want* to become generous; you want to serve, to give yourself away.

Gratitude is the beginner's practice because it's about *you*.

Generosity is the advanced practice because it's not about you; it's about helping others.

Generosity will break your heart. It will heal your Love threshold. You will realize that *everybody needs your love*.

You don't have to love everybody. That's too hard; don't start there. Just begin to notice how much everyone needs and wants to be loved. Let it soften and open your heart.

The more generous you are, the less you worry about yourself. The less attached you are to outcomes. Things will be okay.

[COACHING FROM ESSENCE]

That's advanced gratitude—you're grateful for everything in your life, not just the good things.

And that may lead you to *grace*.

One meaning of grace is *undeserved*. Good fortune. God is looking favorably upon you. Another meaning is *elegance*, moving with *ease and grace*. Another meaning is *kindness and mercy*.

Kindness.

That's a good practice.

What would it be like to coach from a place where you are being kind, from a place of ease?

I was on a quest long before I found my way to coaching from my essence. I had an inkling—before I understood about self-interest, status-seeking, scarcity, and survival, and before my life fell completely apart—that my life was out of alignment. I had no idea about quests then, but I wanted to find a more meaningful way to be in the world.

I thought I might be a healer.

I went to acupuncture college for over three years and passed the California licensing exam. And then never practiced.

That time wasn't entirely wasted.

The most important thing I learned while studying acupuncture didn't come from my teachers. It came from a book I read when I first contemplated going on that journey. The book was *The Web That Has No Weaver* by Ted Kaptchuk. There was a particular passage that captured my imagination—and my heart.

The passage was about an idea called *Penetrating Divine Illumination*.

"Penetrating Divine Illumination," Kaptchuk wrote, "is the ultimate basis of healing."

[THE ULTIMATE PRACTICE]

The ultimate basis of healing.

"Penetrating Divine Illumination is the magic of soul meeting soul, Spirit Reflecting Spirit."

I *love* that.

"The immediate responses of the physician [practitioner] in the clinical encounter—the words, posture, gestures, questions, attention, intention, genuineness, empathy, compassion, belief, and vision—deeply affect and resonate with the Spirit of another human being."

The patient gets better before they're treated. Before they take the medicine.

When people are around you, they feel better.

Aspire to become that kind of person. Before you coach someone, before anything happens—just being with you—they feel better.

Because everybody needs your love.

That is the ultimate practice.

I want to give you a simple way to think about these approaches to practice—gratitude, generosity, and grace.

Do you remember what it was like to learn how to drive?

What did it feel like when you first learned how to drive? Was it exciting? Maybe a little scary? Did you *really* have to concentrate?

What was it like when you got your license? Were you grateful? Were you thankful that you learned how to drive and you weren't scared anymore? Did you have that feeling of excitement, that pleasure of driving? Did you feel *cool*? It felt good to be able to drive.

That's *gratitude*.

Generosity is when it felt so good to drive that you wanted to chauffeur people around. If a friend needed a ride, "Hey, I'll take

[COACHING FROM ESSENCE]

you!" It was so much fun to drive that the desire to drive was overflowing; you couldn't get enough of it.

Grace is when you get in your car, you get where you're going, and you forget how you got there. You didn't have to think about it at all.

If you are coaching now and it's effort, and you're thinking about everything you're doing but you're happy to be coaching, you're in the gratitude phase.

When you stop thinking about yourself, whether or not the client has a breakthrough, and whether or not they'll renew their agreement, you're in the generosity phase as a coach.

As you continue to practice, you'll get to a place where it's more like grace, where you just show up as yourself. You coach from your essence, and at the end of the session, you forget how you got there. And everyone gets something they didn't know they needed and learns something they didn't know they knew.

That's a great coaching conversation.

The word *coach* was originally the word for what we now call a *car*. A coach is a way to help people get where they're going. It's a way to help them get from A to B.

It's a way to get from A to *something better than they can imagine*.

VIII

ENDNOTES

Silent gratitude isn't very much to anyone.
—Gertrude Stein

ENDNOTES

GOOSE IN A BOTTLE

I first came across this koan in Jason Goldberg's book *Prison Break*. It broke my bottle. You can get a free copy from his website, thejasongoldberg.com.

A TO B

I want to be clear that I mean no offense when I use the term bonsai dream. I love Japanese culture (I studied Japanese acupuncture). I even love bonsai.

GRAVITY

For more on the third quarter effect, see http://www.thespacereview.com/article/2683/1. More about the overview effect here: https://en.wikipedia.org/wiki/Overview_effect.

[COACHING FROM ESSENCE]

Read about space stupids here: https://www.bbc.com/future/article/20141007-why-astronauts-get-space-stupid.

YOU ARE THE SOLUTION TO A PROBLEM THAT NO LONGER EXISTS

Michèle Taipale's website is https://sexloveandleadership.com. She's written about perplexities in this blog post: https://sexloveandleadership.com/fighting-the-one-you-love/.

LEVELS OF CREATION

This model is based on logical levels from Gregory Bateson. I was inspired by Robert Dilts, a leader in Neurolinguistic Programming (NLP), who popularized their use and referred to them as NeuroLogical Levels. More here: http://nlpu.com/Articles/LevelsSummary.htm. For a thorough presentation on NeuroLogical Levels, see Dilts's book *From Coach to Awakener*.

OPTIMIZE FOR SERENDIPITY

Read the Splenda story here: https://www.splenda.com/about-splenda/.
  More about the Post-it Note: https://en.wikipedia.org/wiki/Post-it_Note.
  Littlewood's law of miracles: https://science.howstuffworks.com/science-vs-myth/unexplained-phenomena/littlewood-law-miracles.htm.

[ENDNOTES]

HOW TO KNOCK OVER THE EMPIRE STATE BUILDING

Watch an impressive demonstration here: https://www.youtube.com/watch?v=y97rBdSYbkg&t=70s.

FORM AND ESSENCE

The epigraph is often attributed to Einstein, but according to Quote Investigator, the quote is apocryphal. See https://quoteinvestigator.com/2013/04/06/fish-climb/.

FIND YOUR ESSENCE

Hive makes most of the program material available as open source. There are some other valuable resources there, too. Check it out: hive.org.

Recommended reading: *The Drama of the Gifted Child*, or anything by Alice Miller.

THE ESSENTIAL CHOICE

I often frame the choice as between 4S and EAST. I would add love to EAST, but then it would be LEAST. Clients of one of my apprentices, Vanessa Shaw, suggested TALES. I love Vanessa's take on the choice: "For me, the origin story of 4S is *Shame*. And the origin of EAST is *Love*."

[COACHING FROM ESSENCE]

DUCHAMP'S DOOR

See: https://www.ledocument.com/issue-four/peter-suchin-picks-a-fight-with-marcel-duchamp.

This chapter was inspired by a question posed in the Coaching From Essence community forum by Christyna Serrano.

WHAT YOU WERE BORN TO DO

This video of Paul Potts gives me the chills every time I watch it: https://www.youtube.com/watch?v=dnp-8GrHOIk.

THE RED PAPERCLIP

Kyle MacDonald's website is http://oneredpaperclip.blogspot.com.

Reading *The Prosperous Coach* by Steve Chandler and Rich Litvin was bottle-breaking for me. Highly recommended for client creation.

DREAM TOGETHER

See *Loving What Is: Four Questions That Can Change Your Life* by Byron Katie for more about challenging beliefs and asking the question, "Is that true?" I also recommend her book *A Thousand Names for Joy: Living in Harmony with the Way Things Are*.

[ENDNOTES]

BE THE HOST

Triple-loop learning here: https://www.researchgate.net/publication/258171998_The_origins_and_conceptualizations_of_'triple-loop'_learning_A_critical_review.

For more about organizational citizenship behavior, see: https://www.frontiersin.org/articles/10.3389/fpsyg.2020.00758/full.

TURN TOWARD EVERYTHING

"Turn toward everything" is something that the Tibetan teacher, Chögyam Trungpa Rinpoche, often said to his students. See *Never Turn Away: The Buddhist Path Beyond Hope and Fear* by Rigdzin Shikpo.

More about Milarepa here: https://tricycle.org/magazine/demons-mouth/.

For VUCA, check this out: https://hbr.org/2014/01/what-vuca-really-means-for-you.

I've had several suggestions for what the K in FUC*ED might stand for. My favorite is from Michael English: *kerfuffle*.

For the skydiving and ballroom dancing experiments, see *Top Dog: The Science of Winning and Losing* by Po Bronson and Ashley Merryman.

A MAJOR CHORD

The screenplay to *New York, New York* is by Mardik Martin and Earl Mac Rauch. You can watch the scene (in Italian) here: https://www.youtube.com/watch?v=t2YigFgfnpU.

[COACHING FROM ESSENCE]

THE ADVANCED PRACTICE

See the Harvard HealthBeat post on gratitude: https://www.health.harvard.edu/healthbeat/giving-thanks-can-make-you-happier.

THE MOMENT INSIDE THE MOMENT

Naturally, I was extremely curious to listen to this music, "Come Back to Sorrento," which had such a profound effect on Bergantino's patient. Apple Music lists no less than thirty-five renditions. Versions by Dean Martin and Jerry Vale seem popular. I couldn't find a mandolin version, but if you're looking for something that might be a bit more soothing to the soul, try Anthony Vento or Brittni Paiva on guitar.

ACKNOWLEDGMENTS

I started to list all the people who helped me become who I am today, so I could write this book, and the list went back to before I was born. I can't thank enough people, and of the people I thank here, I can't thank them enough.

Thanks to Kat Snow and Shoshana Alexander for coaching and inspiration. Props to Carmen Smith for impeccable editing. One of the privileges of self-publishing is the option to ignore good advice. All of the errors in this book are all mine.

To do work you love with clients you love is a gift. I've been privileged to work with extraordinary clients, too numerous to mention. You know who you are. I'm keeping your secrets.

Monique Giggy gave me the opportunity to present some of these ideas for the leadership track of the Global Startup Program at Singularity University. It was a privilege to teach leadership and coach so many inspiring entrepreneurs working to positively impact a billion people.

My deep gratitude to the Coaching From Essence community and, in particular, to my apprentices: Doug Erwin, Peter Kovacs, Greg Rickman, Vanessa Shaw, Arielle Shnaidman, and Daniel Stillman.

[COACHING FROM ESSENCE]

Erica, Rex, and Hannah Hoffman were with me when I was in a very dark place. Ray Ellis and Sandra Brackert caught me when I was falling. David Buettner, Vlad Moskovski, and Genette Eaton lifted me up. Upeka Bee and Dilan Dane helped me fly (Dilan taught me that everybody needs my love).

For everything and everything, I give Michèle Taipale my naked heart.

THE COACHING FROM ESSENCE PROGRAM

The first coaching From Essence training was held in January 2020. Before COVID-19 turned the world on its head, 21 coaches from as far away as Singapore and Chile met in an Airbnb in Brisbane, south of San Francisco. Over a long weekend, from Thursday evening to Sunday afternoon, they learned how to do powerful work, love what they do, and create practices that would support them financially to do the work they love.

After COVID-19 made it unsafe to meet in person, the program went online, making it available to people worldwide. After several cohorts, the program was made completely free on the Coaching From Essence community forum. You can now watch over a hundred hours of videos, including the complete program, Master Classes, Client Creation Sprints, coaching demonstrations, and more. And it's all completely free.

For more information, visit coachingfromessence.com or @coachingfromessence on YouTube.

ABOUT THE AUTHOR

Robert Ellis is an executive coach and the founder of Futurosity and the Coaching From Essence training program for executive coaches.

Robert has over 35 years of experience working with global companies—spanning startups, mid-stage, Fortune 500 giants, and non-profits— guiding leaders to take their impact to the next level at any stage of growth. His proven strength in coaching entrepreneurs and CEOs to become better leaders, think more strategically, create high-performing teams, foster future-friendly cultures, and deliver compelling presentations—including several high-profile IPO roadshows—has earned him praise from one client as "one of Silicon Valley's best-kept secrets."

He's taught leadership and coached entrepreneurs at Singularity University, and developed and delivered the leadership curriculum for the Global Startup Program.

He was one of the original coaches for the Nasdaq Milestone Maker program, helping late-early to mid-stage entrepreneurs grow their businesses to the next level.

More information at futurosity.com.

Made in the USA
Monee, IL
06 April 2023